VISIONS AND CHIMERAS

L'imagination vit de chimères et de visions

BIZET

VISIONS & CHIMERAS

BY

PROSSER HALL FRYE

BOSTON

MARSHALL JONES COMPANY

MDCCCCXXIX

THE PLIMPTON PRESS · NORWOOD · MASSACHUSETTS
MADE IN THE UNITED STATES OF AMERICA

IN putting together this little collection of essays, I have been guided rather by the merit of the subject than by that of the essay itself. However it may be with the discussion, there is no author or topic discussed which has not some sort of interest or significance still. At the same time these papers, whatever their shortcomings, were all prompted by some particular occasion and had once a kind of pertinence of their own. Though it must be added that the same circumstance to which they owe this one virtue, has too often limited their view of the matters with which they are concerned to a single aspect or phase. At all events I have to thank *The Nation, The Bookman,* and *The Outlook and Independent* for permission to use material that appeared originally in their columns.

CONTENTS

VISIONS AND CHIMERAS

Visions & Chimeras

SHERIDAN

THERE are some characters that seem predestined to serve as the scapegoats of human frivolity. Upon them legend delights to pitch and empty the whole budget of folly which respectability is unwilling to own to in itself but is perfectly ready to chuckle at in others. Such to no small extent seems to have been the *rôle* of Richard Brinsley Sheridan. In this sense story and fable have made so free with his name that it is difficult to tell how much of the current conception of the man is fact and how much is fiction. Hitherto the general reader who would ravel out the skein of tradition, which seems to grow more complicated with every effort to extricate it, has had to rely for the truth upon the biographies of Percy Fitzgerald and Fraser Rae, both of which are unsatisfactory in many respects as finished likenesses, as for that matter is also Walter Sichel's, which aims to correct and complete them. But where is the perfect biographer? And in his absence a cloud of witnesses is not without its advantages; it at least supplies the critic with material for his own conclusions.

I

Sheridan is one of those rare amphibians who live partly in literature, partly in politics; who belong at once to the two elements of imagination and reality. This double *ménage* makes him, like Swift, who is in so far his counterpart, a rather difficult subject of criticism. He is not to be found wholly in his plays or in his speeches — in one sense it is questionable whether he is to be found in both together. He resides in a great measure outside of his professions. He has not a trace of Swift's deadly seriousness. He is at bottom a man of pleasure, to whom these occupations are but expedients — a means to live. In the incorrigible levity of his character he is much like Sterne — only more effectual. His genius is largely an affair of animal spirits, so little does it have to do with the intellectual or moral nature. It is impossible wholly to stifle the suspicion that he is amusing himself even with what purport to be his most serious efforts.

Of such a character you can hardly expect the logical consequence of a fanatic, an idealogue, a man of principles like Burke — any more than you can expect of the stage the solid consistency of life. What stood him in the place of principle or even policy, it would sometimes seem, was a desire to strike the imagination. He was, above all, a social creature, the man of an audience. His first thought is of the play — the illusion, the stage effect. And what an effective, what a brilliant performance it must have been! To know him at his best, it would be necessary to replace him in his original setting, to restore the situation, social and political, in all its intricate intrigue with its conflicting motives and its cross purposes, to recall the vanished actors and set them wheeling again in their rounds of gaiety and self-interest — the captivating Georgiana of Devonshire, the romantic Mrs. Crewe, the generous and profligate Fox, the tinsel "Florizel" of Carlton House, "first gentleman of Europe" and heir apparent to the throne of England. But the old comedy is long since played out to its foregone conclusion, and we are left to imagine as best we can the audacity and fascination of him who was one of its most striking and versatile performers.

And yet though Sheridan realizes himself

fully neither in literature nor in history, he is always oscillating between these two poles; he is constantly manifesting himself in one or the other of these two worlds — he is either the humorist, the man of fancy and invention, or else the statesman and manager, the man of affairs — ever a little too much of the former, no doubt, to make a complete success of the latter. And it is his instability — the unexpectedness with which he shifts his ground so that you never know just where to have him, the persistency with which the one character will be getting into the other's light — which makes him so interesting, and sometimes so unedifying.

It is frankly in the former capacity that he begins his career — with an elopement and two duels. About the whole affair there is something as paradoxical, as quizzical as any of his literary compositions. Whatever the feelings of the parties at the moment, whatever the bunglings of the fate that mislays our prettiest *dénouements,* his elopement is essentially a comic situation, which might serve as a pendant to the scene between Lady Teazle and Joseph Surface — an elopement in all the proprieties, with a duenna in waiting, wherein everything is saved but appearances. And with what waggishness

the penniless lover, who is innocently masquer-
ading as a friend to all concerned, hoodwinks
his rival and contrives that some one else shall
bear the expenses of the frolic! His whole
genius is in it; for the future he has only to
reduce himself to writing.

Nor does his later life belie the mingled jest
and earnestness of his beginnings. He is always
living at loose ends himself, always in arrears,
always behind time, his affairs in hopeless disorder, his letters unread, his appointments un-
met; and yet he aspires to manage a theatre or
two, to control a political party, to direct a
prince, to carry out a national policy. In the
general chaos of his existence he is forever
making shift, with incredible dexterity and
presence of mind, to extricate himself from
difficulties that would never have arisen in the
first place without the grossest tardiness
and negligence. He is admirably cool, good-
humoured, and resourceful. But his abilities are
wasted on temporary expedients — to put off
a dun or wheedle a tradesman or pass off an in-
discretion. His was the dodge by which the
public lie in denial of the Prince's marriage to
Mrs. Fitzherbert was accommodated and the
lady sentimentally reimbursed for the loss of
her character. Even in his moments of power

he is restrained by some refinement of delicacy — a scruple that, however fine, seems more dramatic than political, and calculated rather to meet the needs of the literary imagination than of practical common sense — from securing the advantages for which he has been working all along. In a day of party — a system of things which the conscientious Burke himself defends at length — he had too much of the original about him to become a mere collaborator in other men's schemes. He is incorruptible by his enemies, but he is equally intractable to his friends. Admirable exception as he is to the purchasable politicians of his time, his probity is largely sentimental. It never seems to have crossed his mind that as society is constituted, the management of money is itself a branch of ethics and carelessness of one's own is only a milder kind of dishonesty. If reports are to be believed, he must have practised methodically what Balzac facetiously calls the English system of living on the interest of one's debts. As a result the remark he is said to have made when asked what kind of wine he preferred, would apply equally well to his preference in money — some one else's. About his management of his political credit, too, there is much of the same light-mindedness. After sharing the ill-fortune of the Whigs for years, he finally tricks them out of power by a turn so thoroughly comic that it looks like a caprice of the fancy, an irresistible desire to score a good point at any cost.

In a word, Sheridan combined in his own person the double *rôle* of Joseph and Charles Surface. He had all the former's sophistry of protestation devoid of profound sincerity of conviction, and all the latter's mischievousness of impulse devoid of intentional malice. What evil he did, he expected to excuse, like the one, by the goodness of his heart, and to dignify, like the other, by the elevation of his sentiments. As his father said with reference to "The School for Scandal," "he had but to dip the pencil in his own heart, and he'd find there the characters of both Joseph and Charles." But nature is occasionally more logical than our invention; and it is in significant contradiction with the fallacy of the *dénouement* that he comes to grief in both characters alike. He suffers, not only in the part of Joseph, but also in that of Charles, for his want of seriousness. And yet we must be careful. To take him too seriously is to falsify his proper impression and effect. In a certain large sense he belongs himself to comedy; and while comedy, too, may be a pretty serious business, its seriousness is not that of politics, irresistibly comic as the latter often appears. At all events, it is the former upon which Sheridan's genius has stamped itself most distinctly.

II

The French would probably say, as indeed Taine virtually does, that Sheridan, like the rest of his countrymen, has no sense for comedy at all. But we must take our drama as we find it; and Sheridan's is the very best of anything like genuine comedy that we have. We have a plenty of stage faery and romance, of tragi-comedy and melodrama; but of that sort of exhibition that arouses chiefly amusement and curiosity, which appeals above all to the intelligence, and constitutes something like a *genre tranché* comparable in any degree with the French, we have next to nothing. Congreve and the whole Restoration Comedy have failed to keep the boards for some reason or other — it can hardly be on account of their impropriety, one would infer from the present condition of the theatre. With the possible exception of Goldsmith, who is not in quite the same vein, Sheridan alone survives.

And yet how different is Sheridan himself

from Molière, the representative not only of
French comedy but of the comic spirit at its
fullest and best! It is not merely that he never
wholly rid himself of the fatal English sentimentality, that he never completely parted
company with the muse of lachrymose comedy
against whom he inveighed at his first entrance
upon the scene — though that has a good deal
to do with it too, and accounts for his tenderness for Charles Surface, as it does for his lack
of the absolute intellectual detachment of perfect comedy, the purely disinterested pleasure
in the discernment of character and motive. In
this particular I can not help thinking Charles
Lamb's perceptions less at fault than those of
his critics. But to take the comparison where
it is most favourable to Sheridan — the striking passages in "The Rivals" and "The
School for Scandal," the things by which we
remember Sheridan (I take them as they come)
are phrases like Mrs. Malaprop's "nice derangement of epitaphs" or her "allegory on
the banks of the Nile"; or Sir Lucius O'Trig-
ger's "snug lying in the Abbey"; or Lady
Teazle's "I deny the butler and the coach-
horse"; or best of all, perhaps, Sir Peter's "I
leave my reputation behind me."

But clever as these are, they are not in the

same class with those that leap into mind at the mention of Molière: Orgon's " le pauvre homme! " or Harpagon's " sans dot! " or Argan's "C'est pour moi que je lui donne pour mari ce médicin "; or finally Madelon's " Pour moi, un de mes étonnements c'est que vous ayez pu faire une fille si spirituelle que moi." Decidedly this is quite another thing. It is not cleverness — it is dissection; every stroke disposes of a character. It would be impossible to shift these speeches from one mouth to another, as was Sheridan's habit — a practice that gives much of his dialogue the effect of a uniform veneer. And it is not so much that Molière is greater than Sheridan — or the comparison would be an unfair one — as that he is different. Vastly entertaining as Sheridan is, he belongs with another class — with the wits and the phrase-makers. Like Oscar Wilde he is a producer of smart comedy. " Why don't all these people leave off talking and let the play begin? " asked Jekyll of " The School for Scandal "; and in a word he supplied the formula of the species.

Within these limits, however, Sheridan created the variety. In certain respects the case is much the same with him as with Beaumarchais, whose " Barbier de Séville " came out the same

year as "The Rivals." Beaumarchais may have
been trying, as he pretends, to naturalize and
familiarize the drama; but what strikes us at
first is the conventionality of his intrigues —
the stock motive, the "literary" commonplace
of the plot; it is only later that its perfidious-
ness becomes evident. And so in his own way
with Sheridan; the lover courting his mistress
clandestinely, the hypocrite seducing the wife
of his benefactor — these are not very novel
properties. It is Sheridan's waggery, like Beaumarchais' malice, which saves the situation.
The very quality of his wit is implicated in the
manner in which the triteness of the matter is
turned against itself. To don a disguise in order
to escape discovery by anxious duennas and
guardians, is one thing; it is quite another to
don it, as Captain Absolute does, to conceal
his identity from his mistress herself. To betray
a husband out of passion for some one else,
and to betray a husband, as Lady Teazle con-
templates doing, out of a tenderness for her
own reputation, are two very different things.
So, too, of Joseph and Charles Surface, it would
be difficult to show in what respect the latter is
more virtuous than the former, except in his
contempt for the proprieties. And to much the
same effect the *dénouement* of "The Rivals"

and " The School for Scandal " hinges in both
cases on what amounts to a practical joke, the
duel in the one and the overthrow of the screen
in the other. It is all very English somehow; it
it all good fun. And it is this that makes Sheridan so thoroughly enjoyable. And as a natural
result in his case the better the joke, the better
the play. For this reason " The Rivals " is on
the whole a more successful effort than "The
School for Scandal "— just as Mrs. Malaprop
is the best of his *dramatis personæ* — in spite
of the more finished workmanship of the latter
piece and its greater significance. The former
is more in character, it suited the author better,
and it is, if anything, the happier performance.
In short, it is more fun, just as Sheridan himself is more fun than Congreve, more fun even
than Goldsmith.

III

It is much more difficult to form an estimate
of his oratory than of his drama. Not only has
the taste in eloquence changed almost unrecog-
nizably; most of his speeches exist only in
garbled and mutilated versions as they were
put together from the reporters' memory. In
many cases it is quite impossible to be sure just
what Sheridan said. In others, curiously

enough, the reporters seem to have improved upon the original.

As far as can be judged, however, from what remains, his is what might be called abstract eloquence. It consists very largely in dilating a commonplace by transmitting it through a medium of general and rhetorical terms, which destroy its definition at the same time that they magnify and enlarge it. To be sure, it is a kind of thing of which any ingenious man can produce a passable imitation nowadays, just as he can produce a passable imitation of the verse of the period. But this is not to belittle Sheridan's merit in its discovery or perfection. It seems to have been immensely clever as he did it; and when properly delivered to suit his occasion, it must have been immensely effective too, as it was unanimously applauded — though few of his contemporaries fail at the same time to refer to its artifice and elaboration.

But in justice to this sort of oratory in general and Sheridan's in particular it must still be remembered that those were the good old days of the four and five bottle men, when statesmen gambled and caroused all night, when orators made speeches five and six hours long and fell back exhausted into the arms of their friends, when a public compliment drew forth floods of tears and a public censure streams of vituperation and abuse — the days of sensibility and intemperance, of violence and declamation, when ginger was yet hot in the mouth and men thrived on massive sensations. Even Burke is by no means guiltless of extravagance. And while Sheridan's points seem too often laborious and far-fetched, while he has nothing of his great contemporary's clearness of vision which penetrates at times to the bottom of political institutions and discovers their foundations in the roots of the moral nature itself, yet he has occasionally, at his best, a way of striking words together which produces a very presentable imitation of revelatory lightning. By way of completing my sketch of the playwright and politician I quote a passage from one of these reconstructed speeches for what it is worth.

" An honourable friend of mine . . . has told you that prudence, the first of virtues, can never be used in the cause of vice. . . . But I should doubt whether we can read the history of a Philip of Macedon, a Cæsar, or a Cromwell, without confessing that there have been evil purposes, baneful to the peace and to the rights of men, conducted — if I may not say with prudence and wisdom — yet with awful craft and most successful and commanding subtlety. If, however, I might make a distinction, I should say that it is the proud attempt to mix a variety of lordly crimes that unsettles the prudence of the mind and breeds this distraction of the brain. One master passion, domineering in the breast, may win the faculties of the understanding to advance its purpose and to direct to that object everything that thought or human knowledge can effect; but to succeed it must maintain a solitary despotism in the mind — each rival profligacy must stand aloof or wait in abject vassalage upon its throne. For the power that has not forbade the entrance of evil passions into man's mind has, at least, forbade their union; if they meet they defeat their object, and their conquest, or their attempt at it, is tumult. Turn to the virtues — how different the decree! Formed to connect, to blend, to associate, and to co-operate, bearing the same course, with kindred energies and harmonious sympathy, each perfect in its own lovely sphere, each moving in its wider or more contracted orbit, with different but concentring powers, guided by the same influence of reason, and endeavouring at the same blessed end — the happiness of the individual, the harmony of the species, and the glory of the Creator. In the Vices, on the other hand, it is the discord that insures the defeat; each clamours to be heard in its own barbarous language; each claims the exclusive cunning of the brain; each thwarts and reproaches the other; and even while their full rage assaults with common hate the peace and virtue of the world, the civil war among their own tumultuous legions defeats the purpose of the foul conspiracy. These are the Furies of the mind . . . that unsettle the understanding; these are the Furies that destroy the virtue, Prudence; while the distracted brain and shivered intellect proclaim the tumult that is within, and bear their testimonies from the mouth of God Himself to the foul condition of the heart."

Such is his eloquence. Taken in its context with his other work and considered as a means of deciding the destinies of a great nation, it might seem to constitute a comedy of its own, of which its author was far too clever to be insensible — the comedy of parliamentarianism.

On the whole and however he may look to us nowadays, Sheridan represents what is always a disturbing phenomenon, the irruption of genius into a province usually reserved for other occupants. With posterity Burke has come off lightly, thanks to his caution in editing his own memorials — and besides, Burke was much more of the expert. But outside of his comedy poor Sheridan has always lain at the mercy of the diarists and chroniclers, who have tried him by the measure of an officialism to which he did not belong, and finding him fall short, have cried out upon him for lack of a consistency which is not in his proper character at all — or always, be it said, in their own.

NOW that I am on the subject of comedians I am minded to say a word or two of poor Yorick, suggested by Mr. Cross' edition of that worthy, particularly since the appreciation of Sterne as a writer depends so largely upon a knowledge of Sterne as a man. Indeed, there are few of the great English humorists whose work and life it is so hard to disassociate. Not only is Sterne's literary product small, but it is so whimsical, erratic, and affected as constantly to prick the reader's curiosity about its author. "Tristram Shandy," too, might be a sort of *Aus Meinem Leben,* an elaboration or sublimation of personal experience. There is little of the bold detachment of great creative genius about Sterne. To speak properly, he wears neither tragic nor comic mask; he has merely painted a little for the performance, and the expression — the smirk, the sly grimace, the wink and nod — is still in great measure his own.

It is for this reason that I have referred to Mr. Cross' edition; it is so comprehensive. It collects everything of Sterne's which has so far come to light, including a number of important additions and corrections to what has hitherto been published. In this way it supplies the material for a more intimate and in so far accurate estimate than was formerly possible. The correspondence has been rearranged, and when in error, redated, with some small advantage occasionally to his character. The notorious letter to Lady Percy, for instance, on the strength of which Thackeray accused him of lying to Eliza Draper, has been put back two years, to a time before the beginning of his intimacy with the latter. Forgeries have been weeded out; collateral matter of various kinds, such as John Croft's anecdotes, have been gathered in; and the biography by Percy Fitzgerald has been incorporated. But the most important contribution by far is the Gibbs manuscript, herein for the first time made available to the general reader.

This extremely interesting find is composed almost exclusively of documents in the case of the Mrs. Draper aforesaid; namely, part of a Journal which Sterne kept for her, something in the manner of Swift's for Stella, after her departure for India, together with a disquisition of hers — it would be incorrect to call it an epistle to a friend, dated four years after Sterne's death, and animadverting upon their relationship. If this dreary screed of a hundred octavo pages or thereabout is a specimen of her conversation, it is quite impossible for us nowadays to understand the vaunted Eliza's charm. These papers were in the hands of Thackeray when he wrote his lectures on the English humorists and may have had something to do with the virulence with which he attacks Sterne. At all events they were enough to make Percy Fitzgerald change for the worse his opinion of that vivacious gentleman and rewrite his life accordingly.

And indeed they leave Sterne hardly a rag to drape himself withal. It is not so much their cold-blooded evidence to the nature of his "philanderings," as he euphemistically called them, which is so fatal; it is the fatuity, the looseness and vulgarity of soul that they disclose. In the composition of the Journal, there is no doubt, he drew thriftily and freely upon his love-letters to his wife, "my L." written nearly thirty years before. The literary motives of the two productions are exactly alike. Precisely the same *rôles* are assigned to the two maid-servants, Fanny and Molly, whose office is to feed his flame and flatter his ladies' vanity by ingenuous ejaculations upon the virtues of their absent mistresses. There is the same unnatural exaltation of tone in both, the same sentimental *tic*. And not only this, but the elderly lover of the Journal, whose vein is running pretty thin by this time, refurbishes for the fascination of his new charmer the very phrases with which he wooed that wife for whose death he is now wishing in no very ambiguous terms.

One of these repetends it may not be amiss to quote for it is in the genuine manner of Shandean sentiment, though it gives small notion of the air of sanctimonious seduction breathed by the collection as a whole; and further, as Sterne himself remarks, "the ruling passion, and *les égarements du cœur* are the very things which mark and distinguish a man's character." With the exception that in the first version "My L." occurs for "Eliza" and "Fanny" for "Molly," the two readings are virtually identical.

"5 in the afternoon — I have just been eating my Chicking, sitting over my repast upon it, with Tears — a bitter Sauce — Eliza! but I could eat it with no other — when Molly spread the Table Cloth, my heart fainted

within me — one solitary plate — one knife —
one fork — one Glass! O Eliza! 'twas painfully
distressing, — I gave a thousand pensive penetrating Looks at the Arm Chair thou so often
graced on these quiet, sentimental Repasts —
& sighed & laid down my knife and fork, — &
took out my handkerchief, clap'd it across my
face & wept like a child — "

Lucky for his complacency that he was never
able to read, as we are, his inamorata's last
word, the comment of his perfidy.

" I believed Sterne implicitly, I believed
him! " writes Eliza Draper in the moral essay
already spoken of. " I had no Motive to do
otherwise than believe him just, generous & unhappy — till his Death gave me to know that
he was tainted with the Vices of Injustice,
Meanness & Folly."

So ends the shabby drama.

About the Journal there is, it must be con-
fessed, rather more smoke than fire; it illustrates the curiously factitious heightening, the
sort of literary intensification to which his feeling was, no doubt, liable and which composed
in part the sentimentalism of his age. But at
the same time it is a damning witness to the
final demoralization of the flippant and un-

stable character who composed it. In the words of Chateaubriand, himself no unromantic being, " The poverty of our nature is so great that in our passing infirmities we are able to express our recent affections only in words already used by us in our former attachments. Nevertheless there are words which should be used only once; they are profaned by repetition." Even Percy Fitzgerald in the modified version of his life has very evidently had to make the best of him; and the attentive reader is constantly struck by discrepancies of tone as between the biography and the first-hand pieces which make up the bulk of his work.

From the latter source it would seem to result that the gravest defect of Sterne's character was a lack of sobriety. In practical conscience, in the sense of conduct he was sadly wanting. I do not mean to say that he was unworldly in any interpretation. He understood well enough how to get on in the world — at least, how to get on with it. " I thank God (B——'s excepted) I have never yet made a friend or connection I have forfeited, or done aught to forfeit," he boasts to Stephen Croft. But with Sterne the power of making and keeping friends consisted mainly in the ability to catch a note easily and sustain it, as is usually the case with promiscuous friendships like his. The letters to Hall-Stevenson and those written during his first trip to London in 1760 at the very beginning of his prosperity, are masterpieces in this sort. Strained as were his relations with his wife, he seems to have managed pretty well even with her. That he had engaging qualities can not be gainsaid — vivacity, drollery, good humour, amiability, above all, folly. No one could ever accuse him of having no nonsense about him. The willingness to talk amusing rigmarole will alone carry a man a long way. From Paris, where his popularity was phenomenal, he writes to Garrick, " I Shandy it away fifty times more than I was ever wont, talk more nonsense than ever you heard me talk in all your days " — and " have converted many unto Shandeism."

This is vastly amusing of course. The pity of it is, he lacked so completely the stern Puritanical passion for personal consistency. There have been great men — at least great writers — almost entirely without it. Montaigne could push skepticism to the verge of universal negation and still remain a devout Roman Catholic without a misgiving. But nowadays, when Puritanism pervades the modern consciousness, it is shocking to conceive that one should keep

incompatible beliefs in the various compart-
ments of his mind or should profess other
principles than those he practises. Hypocrisy
has become our satirical target. And besides,
Sterne's levity went even deeper. With the best
will in the world it is impossible to detect any
sort of purpose or conviction in his life. At
times it seems as though he had not even that
mechanical principle of consistency which results from reasonably consecutive states of consciousness. " And if God, for my consolation,"
he writes after one of his visits to London,
" had not poured forth the spirit of Shandeism
into me, which will not suffer me to think two
minutes upon any grave subject, I would else
just now lie down and die — die — and yet in
half an hour's time I shall be as merry as a
monkey — and mischievous too, and forget
it all — so that this is but a copy of the
present train running across my brain." The
ramblingness of "Tristram Shandy" is, of
course, partly affected; but it must have answered to his temper or he would not have
adopted it. Hence, in default of personal integrity, that singular air of factitiousness about
the whole man, noticeable already in the
" Journal to Eliza." In spite of his immanence
in his work, he seems every now and then to

dissolve insubstantially away into his writing as though he himself were only another apparition among the figments of his own fancy.

And there is evidence that he felt it so. He is something besides a *farceur* — something other, we may be pardoned for thinking, than an English Rabelais. Rickety of body, subject to hæmorrhages of the lungs from his youth, addicted to dissipation physical and mental, he must have had terrible moments of reaction in which graver thoughts were bound to haunt him. It is not easy, however, to find explicit utterances of the kind before the last broken months of his life. He had taken his cue partly from the general disposition of his time, partly from his own associates. " Company, villainous company," he might have exclaimed with Falstaff, " hath been the spoil of me! " though it is certain that such society was his preference, as it was Falstaff's. " I resolved from the beginning," so he has recorded, " that if ever the army of martyrs was to be augmented — or a new one raised — I would have no hand in it, one way or t'other." And in an episcopal letter of admonition Bishop Warburton reminds him very pertinently that " one who was no more than even a man of spirit would choose to laugh in good company, where priests and virgins may be present " — a phrase, by the way, at which he has his jibe a little later in " Tristram Shandy." And yet persistently as he played his part, there are occasional hints of weariness and depression both from his own hand and that of his contemporaries. " Sterne never possessed any equal spirits," declares one of the latter, " he was either in the cellar or the garret."

But after all, the clearest evidence to his acedia is his literature. There it is apparent, not merely in the unevenness, but also in the flavour, of the performance, in the pathos or " sentimentality," as he would call it, which gives his writing its peculiar tang. Superficially, Sterne was a humorist as Aristophanes, Rabelais, and Swift were — that is, not only was he something of an oddity himself, but he had the keenest of eyes for human inconsistency and folly. This elemental sense of the ludicrous is by no means squeamish; it is not incompatible, we know, with a good deal of coarseness and vulgarity, so that we are apt to think of it as unshrinking, hearty, and robust. But in Sterne's case it appears to have been tinged with a sort of involuntary misgiving; he belongs to a weaker, punier generation of authorship. Not that his satire is any

more merciful or sympathetic, in reality, than
another's or his mirth more decorous — they
are only the more venomous and salacious, if
anything, for his debility; but they are inter-
rupted every now and then by a spasm of com-
punction, as it were, a sudden recognition of his
own fragility and a realization of helplessness
and exposure, which exasperates the sensibilities and magnifies the petty miseries of life —
the great ones he never touches — out of all proportion. And the statement might stand for the
secular sentimentalism as a whole. That such
moods were not unfamiliar to him at all events
is clear from his last letters, where he writes
of them with an assurance that must have come
from long acquaintance — perhaps, from solitary brooding in his lonely country parish after
the fatigues and excitements of a visit to London. To Hall-Stevenson he writes thus of his
last journey to Coxwould:

" I have got conveyed thus far like a bale of
cadaverous goods consigned to Pluto and company — lying in the bottom of my chaise most
of the rout, upon a large pillow, which I had
the prevoyance to purchase before I set out. . .
I know not what is the matter with me — but
some strange *dérangement* presses hard upon

this machine — still I think it will not be over-
set this bout. My love to G——. We shall all
meet from the east and from the south, and
(as at the last) be happy together."

What a ghastly parody of sprightliness —
and at the same time what a flash of revelation!
It is like a *crise* of the nerves, this sentimentality — a *tic* I have called it. And while the
quotation exaggerates, there is something of
the same contraction about all his pathos —
and it is fairly representative — when not
merely a trick — something strained and un-
naturally dilated, even hysterical — something
literary and artificial but none the less singularly affecting. And it is this mingling of traditional jocularity with modern *défaillance*
which constitutes his distinction as humorist.
For from this curious duplicity of feeling for
the absurdity and pity of life there arises the
peculiar irony which in the midst of pathos and
pleasantry alike pierces almost inadvertently
to the illusion of the whole affair, and seeing
the final indifference of grief and mirth, rises
serenely above both. This or something like it
may be what Goethe had in mind when he said
that " the influence of Sterne's spirit was of the
finest sort; whoever reads him feels at once

well and free; his humour is inimitable and it is not every humour which can set the soul at large." Hardly exact. Nevertheless it is in measure as though Sterne, himself without a moral nature, was compelled involuntarily to become a witness to the vanity of the world in which he had frisked and fribbled so unconscionably. Who knows? He may have done as well as another and taken it only as it deserves. And that, no doubt, is his infirmity — that he knew nothing better. Nor was his end at odds with the mockery of his life and work. The jester of a gay and frivolous society, he died alone in his lodgings in the presence of a footman and a sick-nurse, while his fast and fashionable acquaintances were feasting in a nearby street, and was shuffled away incontinently into an obscure graveyard, whence, it is supposed, his body was promptly snatched and sent to Cambridge for dissection. Such was the end of Yorick. He who had laughed with thousands was followed by two mourners; the one was his publisher, the other is unknown. Had he sought, he could have pointed no better moral, nor one more truly in his own vein of ironical pathos and humour. And it is this higher morality, insensibly involved in his writing as in his experience, which has given him his place and permanence in letters. As he lived much in the manner of his day, his contribution to literature consists less in the discovery or invention of new qualities or powers than in the combination of old ones. Nearly everything he did had been done before by some one or other; for like most original geniuses he borrowed freely. But with this irony of his he transformed English humour and made it capable in the hands of his successors, in Dickens' and Thackeray's, of a moral seriousness it had never before possessed.

CARLYLE

IT seems clear on the very face of it that such a style as Carlyle writes in "Sartor Resartus" and "The French Revolution" could never have come naturally to any man. In other of his writings, such as "Heroes and Hero Worship," the peculiarities that distinguish him are less egregious; but they are pronounced enough to justify the epithet Carlylese. Perhaps it is because "Heroes and Hero Worship" was delivered as lectures that it is on the whole more natural, marking a kind of turning point in Carlyle's composition. In that case there would obviously be less opportunity as less excuse or occasion for elaborating a style excessively — for as a matter of fact that appears the appropriate designation for Carlyle's style quite as much as for Pater's — laboured. I do not mean to say that nature in the shape of temperament and character went for nothing in the making of his style — on the contrary they counted for a great deal; they decided what sort of facture he should give his style while he was about it. For I do mean that his style is factitious; it is the result of a forcing process. It has been teased and tormented quite as much, if not in exactly the same way, as Pater's. And it is not astonishing for one who has felt the strain of reading him, to learn that he wrote with difficulty and at tremendous expense of spirit.

Indeed, there is perhaps no great English writer, with the exception of George Eliot, upon whom the task of writing told so desperately. He is always depressed or extenuated, complaining querulously at one moment and at another out of temper and exasperated. Or at least if there is an author who has suffered more, there is none whose literary worries and anxieties we are so well acquainted with. His letters and reminiscences, his biography and the memorials of his wife, as edited by Froude, are equalled only by Cross' life of George Eliot as a record of the miseries of authorship. No doubt Carlyle had an unhappy disposition; it is a question whether he could have been happy under any circumstances — rich or poor, married or single, as author or hod-carrier. He had a difficult temper, an endless capacity for worry. Exigent to himself, he was merciless to others — a hard if not impossible man to live with. Some exaggeration there probably is

about the matter; but even when all allowance
is made, the story of his married life reads in
Froude like a Saint Patrick's purgatory, a min-
iature hell on earth. But who was the victim?
Assuredly Carlyle was no brute; but undoubtedly he was abstracted, if not distracted, absorbed, over-wrought, and self-tormented —
just the sort of man, as the shrill Miss Jews-
bury exclaimed, who ought not to marry under
any circumstances. Unfortunately her remark
has been taken to imply another sort of dis-
qualification for a union between the sexes and
has exacerbated a controversy already sufficiently bitter between the friends and advo-
cates of the two parties to the match. The fact
is that our sympathies fly too readily to the
woman in cases of marital infelicity. While
Carlyle had his faults, it can not be denied that
his wife on her side was a high-strung, sensitive,
and impulsive woman, who was quick to feel
as slights what were often only absent-minded-
ness and preoccupation and who was particularly susceptible to any lack of deference on
the part of her husband. Besides, she was of a
higher social rank; and what is so inharmoni-
ous as a difference of breeding! Not unlikely
she thought that in marrying him she had con-
descended sufficiently to make sure of his

deference for the rest of her life. But his ignorance and contempt of the conventions and ob-
servances to which she was used must in the
earlier part of their union have proved a source
of grief and mortification to her. It is easier for
a woman to forgive a breach of morals than a
social solecism. She had married him, so she
said, herself, because she had divined his
genius and wished to be the wife of a great man.
But she had failed to foresee the hardships of
such a lot and bitterly she seems to have rued
her decision.

As a matter of fact Carlyle's treatment of his
wife, such has been the unfortunate publicity
given to their married life, has provoked a
spirited and acrimonious controversy, one party
seeking to lay the blame at his door, another
at hers. Into such roily waters it is hardly desirable to venture. But it may be suggested that
the final decision, if there ever is one, will rest
with the answers to two or three general questions. In the first place, has a man a right to
marry a woman whom he has conscientious
scruples against supporting? For that such was
in the main Carlyle's position is clear. He was
willing — nay, eager to marry; he was probably in love — a little dazzled, perhaps, by the
lady's gentility, after the manner of the boor

who detests and admires his superior; but he
was unwilling to make those ordinary com-
promises and transactions with the world
which are necessary to enable a man to get on
with it, to make a decent living and maintain
a respectable position. He hurried his bride
away into some scrubby Scotch wilderness and
refused to make an effort to secure her the service which her ignorance of housekeeping rendered necessary to her health to say nothing
of her comfort and self-respect. But not only
so — a woman can endure a vast amount of
inconvenience under the circumstances — he
had a way of leaving her out of his life. In one
sense she was right in feeling that she was
nothing to him. Save for her housewifery his
work would have been much the same without
her; she neither contributed to it nor partici-
pated in it. It was only when she died that she
became an influence. He never ceased to regret
her then or to accuse himself of her unhappiness — rather unreasonably after all.

For on the other hand, there is another question. Does a man demand too much of his wife
in asking her to go in with him for the best
there is or what he thinks to be the best? Life
is a stern business after all — to most of us a
duty rather than an entertainment; and he who

takes it sternly is not unlikely to come off best in the end. It is not improbable that in going in directly for prosperity, the prize she was always regretting, she would have found that she had been chasing a will-o'-the-wisp. For the pursuit of happiness is a good deal of a wild goose chase; happiness is usually as it happens, incidental and by the way. But at all events and as it was, their marriage was unhappy, as a marriage is likely to be that fails in its main object. And there is something singularly affecting about the thought of the childless, discontented woman dying alone in her carriage in the course of a drive and her atrabilious widower fretting for the remainder of his life over the vexations of the woman who had persisted in taking his career as a personal injury.

In addition to defects of temper Carlyle had also certain physical weaknesses in spite of great constitutional strength — he lived to be over eighty — weaknesses which were probably aggravated by his sedentary life and his conscientious brooding until they reacted upon his moral character and disposition. In particular he had what is to the student the most annoying of fleshly ills, a weak stomach, an infirmity which had been confirmed by his early hardships. Indeed, after his marriage and during

his early life in London he was so poor, thanks
to his own obstinacy, as to be confined to a diet
of oatmeal, which he used to have sent in from
Scotland by the hundredweight. Nor was it
only dyspepsia that ailed him. He would have
taken his work just as hard if he had had the
digestion of an ostrich. There are men who can
not work without loss of tone and temper. And
in Carlyle's case the matter is more curious —
I should be tempted to call it funnier if I were
not restrained by the thought of his own
solemnity — because his message, the one word
that he had to say, the whole gospel he preached,
was the sanctity, the blessedness of work and
the divine mission of heroism. It was the doctrine of deeds that he felt himself called to pro-
mulgate; and at all times, in season and out,
he would be declaiming for the efficiency and
glory of labour as opposed to the idleness and
vanity of talk and protestation, while he himself encumbered an arm chair and made the
welkin ring with wailing and lamentation.
Take a single entry from his journal; it tells
the whole story:

"April 23, 1840. — Work ruined for this
day. Imprudently expressed complaints in the
morning filled all the sky with clouds — por-

tending grave issues? or only inane ones? I am
sick and very miserable. . . My health seems
hardly to improve. I have been throwing my
lectures upon paper — lectures on Heroes. I
know not what will come of them. . . . If I
were a little healthier — ah me! all were well."

What a picture for the humorist — the apostle
of the heroic and the dynamic, the herald of the
superman, quarrelling with his wife in the fore-
noon and coddling himself during the rest of
the day with his diary. The English Nietzsche!
It would require the hand of a Molière, the
author a Hypocondriac and a Misanthrope, to
do the subject justice. Imagine this creature
cast among the scenes of his French Revolution; he who could not make head against one
poor woman, thrown among the viragoes of
Paris!

Such was the man and such in its way was
his work. That his composition cost as much
pain and kept its author in much hotter water
than Pater's, is certain. Expression was as hard,
at least as laborious for the one as for the other.
And it is worth while to stop a moment for such
a comparison; because it serves to illustrate
two kinds of artificiality in literature; one of
which is too likely to pass as art, the other as

strength. The care which Carlyle gives his work is evidently quite another care than that which Pater gives his. While the impression of Pater's prose is studied, elaborate, painstaking, there is about it an air of calm deliberation, a kind of glacial calm. It is scholarly, academic, subtle, refined or *raffiné*, sophisticated. Written like a dead or at least like a learned language, it has itself something of the fixity and finality, something too of the rigidity and phosphorescence of death. But Carlyle's is boisterous, breathless, hysterical; it is a hurly-burly, though its rough and tumble is no more that of nature than is Pater's frozen quiescence. It is rather the vociferousness of a man working himself to the sticking point, galvanizing himself into a state of frenzied animation with cries and gesticulations, a kind of berseker inspiration. It is like the eloquence of a man with a weak cause. In a manner Carlyle's style suggests the efforts of a regimental band to fire the soldiers with martial ardour; it attempts to supply something wanting or to elevate to the proper pitch something that is of itself unequal to the occasion. For my part I feel as though this blare of trumpets, screaming of fifes, and rattle of drums were calculated to eke out a deficiency or reinforce a note of whose effect Carlyle was more than a little doubtful. I feel, I must confess, as though it was intended to mask a poverty of ideas or a lack of conviction — and yet Carlyle was one of the most positive of men; those who are not quite sure are always the most positive — or say, a lack of genius, the genius which is sufficient to give a subject its proper interest without exaggeration or overemphasis. Essentially it is the falsity of the thing that arouses suspicion, a falsity that has been revealed long since in his " French Revolution."

I may be wrong, very likely I am; and yet as a matter of fact, not only does Carlyle write in this general way, but his range is decidedly limited. His sympathies are narrow and one-sided. He has little or no tolerance. He is moved by resentment more often than enthusiasm. In fact, indignation may be said to be his main spring. Of most of his contemporaries he is uniformly censorious. Wordsworth is " a genuine kind of man, but intrinsically a small one." Macaulay is " at bottom " but " a poor creature with his dictionary literature and erudition, his saloon arrogance. He has no vision in him." Of George Sand he says, " In the world there are few sadder, sicklier phenomena for me than George Sand and the response she meets with."

The poor old poet Rogers is "a most sorrowful, distressing, distracted old phenomenon, hovering over the ruin of deep eternities with nothing but light babble, fatuity, vanity, and the frostiest London wit in his mouth. Sometimes I feel as if I could throttle him, the poor old wretch!"

Even of his friends and intimates he is severely critical. The person for whom he has the most unreserved admiration and affection and with whom he gets along best is his mother. In the evenings they go out into the garden and smoke a quiet pipe together in congenial companionship. With Tennyson too he takes tobacco with some degree of satisfaction for a time, though he soon begins to fear that the poet is in danger of being led astray by popularity.

Contemporary measures he condemns as lavishly as contemporary men. He laughs at our attempts to abolish slavery and writes in ridicule of it. Of our democratic idea he says pithily that "the Radical creed of liberty, equality, and government by majority of votes [is] the most absurd superstition which has ever haunted the human imagination — at least outside Africa." Nor has he Shakespeare's large and curious gaze and open interest in the life about him. It excites his ire; he wants to fight and lame it. At all events he is sure that something ought to be done about it. That man alone who has done something and done something violent about it in any age meets with his indulgence. Just what is to be done about it in his own time he is not quite sure; the virtue lies in the doing and not in the knowing. And so he sits at home and vociferates at the top of his voice that something ought to be done. Even the poet he tries to convert from a maker into a kind of doer; at best the poet furnishes the motives, the ideas for action.

This, then, is his great man, his hero — the man who has done something about it. In this way all progress — for doing something about it he thinks to be necessarily progress — all progress is the work of great men and heroes; for this was before the days when " social forces " were supposed to be the springs of advancement. And perhaps for us who live in these latter days this is the most significant message that Carlyle has still to deliver. For I for one find it a hard saying that society as a whole develops independently of the individual. And I find equal difficulty in believing in any such ontological entity or substance as a " social organism." Society is still as it always has been a company of individuals, whose advance is an affair of individual initiative. The term social organism or whatever equivalent expression the sociological mystics like to use is a mere abstraction still like vitalism or entelechy or what not — *vermöge eines Vermögens.* But at all events such is Carlyle's conception of the hero and his mission — the man who has done something about it and upon whom the well-being of the community consequently depends.

And to reverse the medal, this too is after all his main source of weakness with reference to posterity — the reason probably that he is likely to be so short-lived, if indeed his influence is not dead already. He has done so little, next to nothing — in spite of his insistence upon the individual — for human culture. The basis of our culture is Greek; but he neither derives from it nor reaches his hand to it. His inspiration is from elsewhere and of another sort. In large part at least it is Hebraic. In studying Carlyle it is impossible to forget that he was a Scotch peasant. Both of these origins are important, but naturally the Scotch more than the peasant — though he never got the peasant thoroughly out of him either. In this respect his remarks on Lamb are an edifying illustration of the quality of his grain: —

"November 2. — How few people speak Truth for Truth's sake, even in its humblest modes! I return from Enfield, where I have seen Lamb etc., etc. Not one of that class will tell you a straightforward story or even a credible one about any matter under the sun. All must be packed up into epigrammatic contrasts, startling exaggerations, claptraps that will get a plaudit from the galleries. . . . Wearisome, inexpressibly wearisome to me is that sort of clatter. . . . It is not bounding and frisking in graceful, natural joy; it is dancing — a St. Vitus's dance. Heigh ho! Charles Lamb I sincerely believe to be in some considerable degree insane. A more pitiful, ricketty, gasping, staggering, stammering Tomfool I do not know. He is witty by denying truisms and abjuring good manners. His speech wriggles hither and thither with an incessant painful fluctuation, not an opinion in it, or a phrase that you can thank him for — more like a convulsion fit than a natural systole and diastole. . . . Poor Lamb! Poor England, when such a despicable abortion is named genius! He said there are just two things I regret in England's history: first, that Guy Fawke's plot did not take effect (there would have been so glorious an *explosion*); second, that the Royalists did not hang Milton (then we might have laughed at them), etc., etc. Armer Teufel! "

How wide of the mark this criticism of Lamb is! How completely it misses the point! How misplaced its indignation! It is like quarrelling with a butterfly because you can not make a meal off of it. The fact is that Carlyle had in him from his peasant origin the undying roots of the things he most hated — cant and Philistinism.

But even more important than his social class for his point of view is his nationality. About the Scotch Heine makes in his fleering way a singularly shrewd observation. " Are not the Protestant Scotch," he asks, "Hebrews? Their names sound biblical, their cant Jerusalemitish, and their Religion is a Judaism which eats pork." Flippant as the tone of the remark, the idea itself is suggestive. There is much in Carlyle that recalls after a fashion the minor prophets — his intractable temper, his vehemence, his denunciatory declamation, even his turn of phrase, this censoriousness by which his strictures of Lamb are characterized. Nothing could be more significant in this respect than the difference between his religious utterances and Samuel Johnson's. About the latter there is a sincerity and a massiveness, about the former a turgidness and nasality which are very striking in contrast. There is, indeed, all the difference of dissent and conformity between the two. Johnson's are in the spirit of a great tradition, Carlyle's in that of a fractious and extravagant protest. And it is on account of this immoderation and eccentricity that I say Carlyle's inspiration was Hebraic rather then Hellenic.

On its good side and at its best Hebraism, we are told, is marked by its severe insistence upon righteousness — of a certain sort. It is from the Hebrews that the world has got its taste for formalism as far as it has any such taste. And the weakness of Hebraism, aside from its fondness for covenants and its sense for the canniness of a good bargain, consists in its disposition to insist upon conduct without regarding very closely its reasons and motives. Now, conduct, or action as Carlyle calls it, is no doubt a very important matter — perhaps, the most important of all matters. And on that account the manner in which we should behave ought to be one of the first questions with us. But while undertaking to answer this question Hebraism has always regarded too exclusively the nature of the act alone without examining either its intention or purpose or end. Hence the innumerable ceremonies which a Hebrew had to perform. His day was full of them; he could hardly remember them all; and yet if he forgot one, he was obnoxious to the law. The case was very much like that of our American protestant legislation, for there is a strong dose of Hebraism in all Protestantism. In this way man comes to act by prescription rather than principle. He develops no theory or philosophy of conduct. He never thinks what it were well for man to do. In short, he has no morality. He considers like Carlyle that the act alone is important or momentous; the act clears the score.

But it was just this matter that Hebraism disregarded which Hellenism occupied itself with and which culture has continued; namely, the proper object of action and the right motives of conduct. And withal that culture came to cultivate a regard for intentions: while it hesitated to condemn a man for unfortunate results that he never could have foreseen, it required at the same time that he should act with an eye to the probable consequences of his act: not action but intelligent action was the recommendation. Better not to act at all than to act without sufficient light. And culture is nothing more than the philosophy, if you please, which human experience and wisdom have developed with respect to these affairs. But to this philosophy Carlyle contributed next to nothing — naturally, since he refused to accept it at all — insisting rather upon the virtue of the act as such and having little or nothing to say about its quality or character. " Attempt not the impossibility ' to know thyself,' but solely ' to know what thou canst work at.' " No more un-Hellenic words were ever uttered. The fact is that it does make a difference what you are doing and what your grounds are for doing it, and it does make a difference too what you are; and in neglecting such a rudimentary and obvious truth, Carlyle could hardly help building on a sandy foundation.

Under these circumstances his admiration for Goethe seems rather curious. As a whole his interest in German literature is intelligible enough. He was probably attracted by its formlessness and vagueness. There was little of the artist about Carlyle. He denies himself any turn for *Kunst,* as he calls it. That is the one human business that he can not understand. And the formlessness, the unplasticity of German, so far from offending, actually fascinated him. But with Goethe it is another matter. Goethe was concerned not only for art but for contemplation as well. In spite of the hugger-muggery of " Wilhelm Meister " there is finally a lucidity, a directness, an immediate penetration about Goethe's mind which is foreign to Carlyle's. And so when you come to think of it, you find that it is the Goethe of romance, the Goethe of " Wilhelm Meister " whom Carlyle affects.

Finally, when all is said and done — for his individualism is too impure and amounts to no more than an egotism of personal assertion — the most satisfactory trait of Carlyle's thought is his pessimism. As far as he can be saved at all, it is his pessimism that saves him. He had no disposition to deny a certain range of facts which are perfectly patent but which are so unpalatable to official and private optimism that they seldom secure recognition. And it is remarkable that the nearest Carlyle comes to seeing things as they are, is in such cases as this. Society is always hollow; its members are always wretched. Life is ever miserable; happiness is but an illusion. The only knowledge that is of any account is that which enables us to distinguish truth from error, to dispel our own hallucinations, and to endure the hardships of our lot. The substitution of comfort for religion and philosophy is a step in the wrong direction because it enervates the mind and inculcates the utterly false idea that life might be happy under favourable circumstances. "He [Hunt] has a theory that the world is, or should, and shall be, a ginger-bread lubberland, where evil shall never come: a theory in very considerable favour here, which to me is pleasant as streams of unambrosial dishwater, a theory I simply *shut my mouth* against as the shortest way."

So much for his ideas. As for his "genius," he does not appear, great man as he was, to possess that transcendant faculty which is so inspired by its themes as to make them inspiring to others without strain and effort. When a man is doing work to which his powers are fully adequate, when he has come to know himself and is acting on that knowledge, he does not make all this pother about it. But Carlyle — he seems never to see his subject true; certainly, he seldom writes it so. He is looking at things through the big or little end of his telescope. Nor does he wield the language like a master. He rides to be sure, but he kills too many horses under him. Hardly a sentence in which he does not do violence to the instrument that he is using. Shakespeare, of course, has his violences too; but they are accidental, they are not essential to his best effects. Whereas in Carlyle they are; they occur in his most characteristic passages and it is they very largely for which we read him; for as a matter of fact they do tickle or shock our jaded attention. His idea in writing " Sartor Resartus," which is the most startling thing that he ever did, was avowedly to call attention to himself. He wished to wake up too some morning and find himself famous. He felt rightly or wrongly that the time was come for his name to be known. And so he attempted a *tour de force*, distrusting the effectiveness of a more legitimate style. But alas for his anticipations! " Sartor Resartus " stood him in for little fame or money. But at all events something of this same distrust of the legitimate means and manner of expression seems to have haunted him all his life. It is as though he were afraid to put forth a subject on its own merits, but must create a factitious interest, a crowing and cackling in the barn yard so that every one should be convinced of its importance. In reality a great many of his wonderments, pregnant questions, mystifications, gnomic utterances are mere forms of words. "Where is to-morrow resident even now? " Such verbalisms are not only vague; they are nonsensical. Occasionally it is possible to catch him in the very act of bolstering out a sentence into a *sententia* with meaningless vocables — mouthing his phrases, as it were — not so patently, of course, in his deliberate writing where he had to disguise his *procédé* as in his letters and diaries where he unwittingly betrays himself. " However by the strength of men's heads and arms a mighty improvement is and will be accomplished." Or perhaps in his state of mind — sedentary and melancholic as he was — he may not have had sufficient interest in his subject himself to do his best with it but must needs work himself up by such means as we are all familiar with, as a sluggish appetite requires to be quickened with condiments.

" There is no idler, sadder, quieter, more *ghostlike* man in the world even now than I. Most weary, flat, stale seem to me all the electioneerings, and screechings, and jibberings, that the earth is filled with, in these or indeed any days. Men's very sorrows and the tears one's heart weeps when the eye is dry, what is in that either? "

Something of all these causes was at work in his language, no doubt; and yet his temperament had much to do with the result too. He was excitable when once aroused. Not only was he nervously irritable — I have no doubt that things seemed bigger, louder, and redder to him than to ordinary men, when they struck his attention at all. "There was one of those guardians there," he writes of a watchman in the streets of Edinburgh, " whose throat I could have cut that night; his voice was loud, hideous, and ear and soul piercing, resembling the voices of ten-thousand gib-cats all molten into one terrific peal." He suffered horrors from sleeplessness — the ordinary noises of the night were monstrous in his ears; even the crowing of the cocks threw him into paroxysms of fury, and not the least of his wife's trials consisted in suppressing the neighbours' hens and dogs. Not only that, I say, but in addition when once stirred, he fell into a mental frenzy too. He had that combination of initial inertia and eventual excitability which is frequently characteristic of the sedentary student or thinker. The experience is not unfamiliar. After long brooding on a subject there comes a moment when the mind becomes stultified and inept. The innumerable details of the subject, the multitude of ideas suggested in connection with it, appear to overpower and confound the mind — an effect which is aggravated by the silent and solitary study and by the tedium and strain of concentration. The mind is inert and listless. But if this sluggishness is once overcome, before it settles into the apathy of discouragement, then it often happens that a state of intellectual excitement is induced by force of the very same causes that were responsible for its predecessor. Ideas hurry and jostle in the mind; the hand can hardly keep up with the head; the thought outruns the pen; and there results an impatience, a feeling of haste and agitation, while the brain warms more and more to the work and the expression becomes more and more vivid and high-coloured, just as a man in a passion grows louder and louder, more and more vehement and voluble, more emphatic and abusive as he proceeds. So it is that one and the same person may have known the necessity for galvanizing himself into interest and yet once started may have been carried away by his own factitious impetuosity. Indeed, it seems at times as though Carlyle could not shout loud enough to give his utterances the importance which in his hypersensibility he thought they deserved. And hence, very probably, his distrust for plain statement as quite inadequate to convey the final irritability of his feelings.

It happens frequently that a book or an author comes to be associated in our minds with some recollection which does not appear at first sight very congruous with the subject but which has a kind of remotely illustrative or symbolic value. For my part the older I grow the harder it is for me to make any very sharp distinction between my own memories and my reading. Not that one is in danger actually of confounding the two; but only that they seem about equally real or equally illusory. And so the association once made becomes all the easier and more natural.

About a mile out of the village where I was brought up, the old Boston turnpike runs over a long hill and into an avenue lined with willows. In the middle of this stretch of road a lane used to open through the fields and ascend a slope or ridge of ground to a dilapidated farm-house and its straggling out-buildings. The house stood in a kind of plantation of trees and the lane itself was screened with elms, firs, and underbrush. Here lived old Dan Harding, alone on the shabby run-down homestead which had belonged to his fathers ever since there was a town. In deference to his character he was generally known among the townsfolk as Black Dan; and there was a kind of superstition connected with his name among the youth of the neighbourhood as of one who had sold himself to the devil. As a matter of fact I never heard anything definite about the transaction or indeed about any of the other nefarious businesses in which he was popularly supposed to have a hand. But the very vagueness of his reputation only invested him with the greater awe in my boyish imagination.

One thing, however, was certain, for I had seen it myself. Of moon-lit nights there was a kind of lunacy came upon Black Dan. Now and then of a bright summer night when the moon was up, I have passed the lane that led to his house, and felt my blood run cold as I heard his shrieks ripping up the shadows and saw at intervals his fantastic figure emerge from the gloom of the little grove about the house and flit across a patch of lighted ground, capering and gesticulating, snapping his fingers at the moon and abusing it with horrid curses and imprecations in a crescendo of fury and exasperation. Once or twice I yielded to the uncanny fascination of the performance and ventured to creep a little closer, up the dark lane, with a palpitating heart, in expectation of immediate discovery and annihilation; for I had no means of knowing how many of my secrets a man who stood in such confidential relations with the moon might be possessed of.

On my own side I had a dim hope that if I could get near enough to hear him distinctly, I might surprise his secret, for that there was a mystery about the matter I was convinced — and how did I know that he was not practising some powerful incantation? But I never went far enough to find out. The tension of my fears, increasing like a spring the farther I crept, always overpowered my curiosity at some point too remote for my purpose. And I have since had reason to suppose that the only spirit he conjured with was Medford rum, which was the familiar of the Yankee farmer in those days. But prosaic as it all seems now, I shall never forget the impression of portentous significance that I used to feel, on the Boston turnpike, amid the gloom of the willows, in listening to Black Dan raving maniacally at the moon, who went her habitual rounds just as usual.

The analogy seems preposterous. I should be the last to compare Carlyle with my New England dervish; but nevertheless the two are associated in my thoughts. I can not help feeling in Carlyle something of that pointless frenzy that used to stir me so powerfully and so vaguely in those other situations, something of that intense excitement about nothing in particular or at least something so indefinite that it can not be named, an exasperation of the nerves. And yet even now, when I sit down to read " Sartor Resartus " as I have just been doing, I can not wholly rid myself of the belief or superstition that there is something there somewhere — some charm or magic, some powerful spell which I might surprise if I could only get at it and with which I might conjure spirits and not impossibly read the riddle of life. But alas! the task is too great for me; for me the mystery remains impenetrable.

Matthew Arnold

MATTHEW ARNOLD is by all odds the most considerable critic in English. To be sure English criticism is by no means the best in the world. It is immeasurably inferior to French. And at the same time that it has no name to rival Sainte-Beuve's, it is also without any such single exceptional manifestation of critical genius as was Goethe during the latter part of his life, though it must be added that Goethe was a critic only incidentally and by odds and ends, not systematically and by profession. In the main, however, English criticism is superior to German; and though not of the very first order on an average, has never been lacking in able and distinguished practitioners of the second rank, like Dryden, Hazlitt, and Coleridge, men not wholly incomparable with their French competitors, Bossu, if not Boileau, La Harpe, Vinet. Of all these, however, Matthew Arnold is undoubtedly the greatest, the one who comes nearest to equalling the best of the French even if he does not quite do so.

From such an appraisal, nevertheless, a great deal of Matthew Arnold's work must be excepted. His writings on specifically religious subjects in particular, although they may contain some shrewd and pertinent observations, are on the whole examples of mistaken and misdirected energy. " Literature and Dogma," " God and the Bible," " Saint Paul and Protestantism " are rather drawbacks to his reputation as a critic and had in their time the further disadvantage of distracting his own and his reader's attention without benefit to either. They may be dismissed not unjustly with Renan's remark on Philo Judæus, who, he says, was the first to give us an example " of an attempt which was to be often repeated to reduce Judaism to a sort of natural religion or deism by attenuating the portion of revelation and presenting the prescriptions of the Thora as simple precepts of natural reason or hygiene. In such a manner of presenting things revelation is not denied but dissimulated. The Christian apologists after the fashion of Minucius Felix will practise the same method; the apologists of our day abuse it. They diminish the size of the pill to make it more palatable. No scientific mind will ever allow himself to be deceived by these sophisms; but hybrid theses

have often a kind of seduction for the literary."
With these exceptions and taken in his own
field where he belongs, Arnold's superiority to
the run of English critics is unquestionable.

And it is due to a single cause. His criticism
is finally a criticism of ideas. It is not confined
to the observation and analysis of any one particular case, nor is it satisfied with character-
izing the author or the work immediately under
the critic's eyes, as Sainte-Beuve's so often is.
It is, rather, concerned to elicit something general and exemplary, susceptible of a wide application to other subjects and capable at the
same time of serving as a standard or gauge
of literature as a whole. Indeed, his subject
itself seems often but an occasion for considerations of this nature. So with his " Wordsworth " — as compared, for instance, with
Pater's — he by no means contents himself
with an account of the poet and his poetry; it
is the essence of poetry in itself with which he
has to do. And far and away the most significant
portion of the essay is that in which he dem-
onstrates his favourite proposition, " poetry
is a criticism of life."

Even when he deals with a concrete case,
the case itself becomes in some manner typical
and representative in his hands. It is no longer

a mere isolated fact, unique and singular; it has taken on the aspect of a specimen, a sample of something broader still — a tendency, a quality, an aim of some sort. In his essay, "The Study of Poetry" he undertakes no definition of poetry as such, but he recommends, as a "help for discovering what poetry belongs to the class of the truly excellent," the practice of bearing in mind "lines and expressions of the great masters" and applying them "as a touch-stone to other poetry." And he cites several such lines and passages, among them Hamlet's adjuration:

" If thou did'st ever hold me in thy heart,
Absent thee from felicity awhile,
And in this harsh world draw thy breath in pain
To tell my story,"

where the particular instance assumes a kind of general and essential significance, standing for a whole order and range of phenomena and en-abling one to recognize the abstract type of poetry as it were intuitively or sympathetically. For thus much of Plato at least he has in him; he sees the essence in the idea and not in the individual.

So in the comparison of his and Pater's "Wordsworth" which I have just suggested.

For Pater Wordsworth is evidently unique, without a counterpart in the wide world; and his critic's main business is so to characterize him that he will resemble no one else. It is his idiosyncrasy that Pater seeks to catch and confine. In Matthew Arnold's case, however, Wordsworth is a poet, a very great and original poet to be sure, but still, as a poet, a being in whom the laws and the nature of poetry are illustrated, and illustrated only the better and the more purely as he is the better poet — just as the finer the horse, the better he may be supposed to illustrate equine nature, though the more unlike he is to the general run of horses. Both are legitimate points of view; the one Platonic, the other Aristotelian; and while Pater takes the latter, Arnold takes the former, each being for the nonce a little out of his official character. While to Pater the greater the poet, the more exceptional and singular he is; to Arnold the greater the poet, the more typical and illustrative poetically he becomes.

In some such way too as Matthew Arnold discusses poetry in his " Wordsworth " so in " The Literary Influence of Academies " he discusses classic prose; in " Celtic Literature " poetic style in general; in " Translating Homer " the grand style in poetry; in " Culture and Anarchy," culture or humanism; and so on. There is always the special subject, pressed more or less closely but serving as an occasion for something more abstract and fundamental; for it is in the possession of such a body of general considerations and their application to a variety of cases, all apparently diverse but all in reality falling under a common classification, that criticism for Matthew Arnold consists. In short, criticism, so he thinks though he does not say so in so many words, is an affair of principles.

His own definition, to be sure, does not exactly tally with this form of expression; but in reading Arnold, one must remember that he always concerns himself with the spirit of his subject rather than for its method. So, when he says of poetry that it is a criticism of life, he is thinking of the spirit of poetry, not of its method, for in the latter sense the statement would be obviously false. And though he adds somewhere that poetry is, indeed, a criticism of life " under the conditions fixed for such a criticism by the laws of poetic truth and poetic beauty," yet it is characteristic that he should stress in every instance the former part of the definition and leave the latter undeveloped. I confess that for my part I should like to know what these laws of poetic truth and poetic beauty are; but he nowhere specifies them. And so when he says that the business of criticism is "simply to know the best that is known and thought in the world," he is evidently thinking of its inspiration and not of its mechanism. What he has in mind, as his own practice illustrates, is such a knowledge of things that the critic is able to form for himself some kind of sound judgment and taste in such matters as he undertakes to arbitrate and so is able to furnish, in connection with them, good and sufficient reasons for his conclusions. He does not imply that the critic's standard should be inflexible; rather, he recommends Montaigne's measure of lead. "He may retain all his principles; principles endure, circumstances change; absolute success is one thing; relative success another. Relative success may take place under the most diverse conditions; and it is in appreciating the good in even relative success, it is in taking into account the change of circumstances, that the critic's judgment is tested, that his versatility must display itself." But while he would not assimilate the principles of criticism in any way to the laws of science, which are impersonal and irrational, and while he would allow room for the appreciation which recognizes a good thing as it were intuitively and by the force of its own nature; still unlike Pater, he would make that appreciation consist in something other than a set of exquisite sensations and flattering titillations. And he has made this point for himself in quoting Sainte-Beuve with approval. " ' In France,' says M. Sainte-Beuve, ' the first consideration for us is not whether we are amused and pleased by a work of art or mind, nor is it whether we are touched by it. What we seek above all to learn, is whether *we were right* in being amused with it and in applauding it, and in being moved by it.' " There is the gist of the matter. Criticism is not a science but a judgment; it is a reasoned opinion and involves an application of principles.

As Arnold conceived it, he would probably subsume it plausibly enough under the head of conduct — that sort of inferior but not undesirable knowledge which enables us to find our way home. And in fact what is my attitude toward a book or any other subject of decision but a part of behaviour? And in conduct some of us are undeniably to a greater or less extent guided by principles. In ordinary affairs we apply these principles — some of which we have been taught in the form of commonplaces and maxims and others of which we have acquired for ourselves without formulation — almost instinctively and heedlessly as a matter of routine or habit. But in cases of doubt and perplexity we become conscious of a process of generalization and inference. And while there is nothing rigid about such standards, yet if our action is called in question, we are able to rationalize it by exhibiting its grounds and considerations.

Nor do I see that Arnold's criticism is of another procedure. He has, of course, unusual gifts for his work. He has taste. But taste, while partly innate, requires training, " the severe discipline necessary for all real culture," for taste, after all, is a comparative faculty and consists in great measure in distinguishing the good from the inferior, in setting one thing beside another and discriminating between them. In fact, what is taste but discrimination? The critic is the man who knows the difference. We may as well grant that not all are equally endowed with taste as all are not born mathematicians or engineers. But without cultivation even the well endowed are able to make little or nothing of their gifts. And in Arnold's view the education which serves to bring out the natural endowments of the critical character is culture. I say the natural endowments of the critical character because in Arnold's sense culture itself is only a kind of training in criticism.

It must have struck any attentive reader that his definitions of criticism, of poetry, and of culture are singularly alike. " Poetry," he declares in one place, " is a criticism of life." " The business of criticism," he says elsewhere, " is to know the best that is known and thought in the world." And enlarging upon this statement, he concludes that " culture is a pursuit of our total perfection by means of getting to know, on all the matters which most concern us, the best which has been thought and said in the world; and through this knowledge, turning a stream of fresh and free thought upon our stock notions and habits." In short, culture and poetry are merely two different applications of the critical spirit. Culture is criticism turned upon the conduct of life and poetry is criticism turned upon the spectacle of life with a view to its representation. The aim of culture is to understand what we are about; the aim of poetry is to interpret the various forms in which human activity manifests itself. " The grand business of modern poetry," to quote his own words, is " a moral interpretation, from an independent point of view, of man and the world." And this curious resemblance or identity — for so it strikes us at first — between culture, poetry, and criticism is inherent in Arnold's conception of criticism. For if criticism consists in the formation and application of general ideas, then it is clear that criticism applies to life and conduct as a whole, as far as life and conduct are intelligible; that is, as fas as they are subjects to be understood. And that they are so in the main can not be doubted. Even our feelings and emotions are to be understood, romanticism notwithstanding; and we recognize as educated that man who does understand himself and that man as uneducated who does not. Culture, then, consists for Arnold in enlightenment, and so does poetry.

Such is his reason for that study of literature which has been so much insisted upon of late and often so unintelligently. Properly studied literature is one of the best means of enlightenment with regard to what we are in the habit of calling rather vaguely life and the world. It is the best means of developing and training the critical spirit. As a matter of fact, whether the physical world around us is organized or not, whether or not it exists, so to speak, ready-made; the moral world at all events, the world of human nature does not. That world man must order, if not create, for himself. " Other creatures submissively follow the law of their nature; man alone has an impulse leading him to set up some other law to control the bent of his nature." Our moral ideas, our principles of conduct, our sense of right and wrong, in a word, our civilization, have been the result of a long and slow development or process of discovery, to which every generation has contributed its quota. Gradually we come to see in what our best activity consists, we disentangle what is proper to man from what is proper to brute, we classify and distinguish, and so we grow slowly and falteringly to a consciousness of ourselves and of our powers. It is all nebulous enough at best; but certain forms we see and prefer. Such is our culture in the sense of possession; it is a composition of many hands and many ages; and it depends mainly upon the continuity of our literary tradition.

By his general conception of criticism, then, and by the relation which it institutes between culture and literature and life, Matthew Arnold's writing gains a kind of solidarity which most critical writing lacks. No matter to what subject he applies himself, his method, his point of view, and his aim are always the same.

Whether it be society, politics, religion, or poetry that he is discussing, his procedure is uniform — an application to the subject of those general principles or ideas about life that he has formed by reading and reflection.

To be sure, these general ideas are not very numerous or always of his own origination — naturally, though I am frequently astonished, unreasonably enough, on analysing an author, to see, as a rule, with what a small stock of ideas he manages to do business. Half a dozen general principles in a broad sense seem a large outfit for any writer. And after all why not? Since the writer's business from the very nature of the case consists in the application and illustration of a few ideas in a great variety of instances rather than in the formation of a great number of ideas. But it is, perhaps, or certainly it seems a more serious derogation to a critic's reputation that his ideas should be second-hand. And this is a charge to which Matthew Arnold lies wide open; it is consistently involved in his notion of culture and criticism. His " Sweetness and Light," as he remarks himself, owes at least its suggestion to Swift. His "Hebraism and Hellenism" takes up an *aperçu* of Heine's, who observes in his essay on Börne: " In this connection I may say that all men are either Jews or Hellenes — men with ascetic, art-hating, ghostly seeking impulses, or men proud of their culture, glad of life, and sensible of reality." To be sure, Arnold has given this hint an extension quite foreign to Heine. But in much the same way any one of any reading at all is likely to find clues here and there in literature to many of his most original ideas. So Girard, the Greek scholar, has an essay on Alexandrianism, in which Theocritus' idylls are spoken of to much the same effect as Arnold speaks of them in his " Pagan and Mediæval Religious Sentiment." Most of all, however, he is indebted to Sainte-Beuve, whom not only does he quote frequently but on whom he has to some considerable extent formed his spirit. In particular does he seem to owe to Sainte-Beuve's essay on Madame de Caylus his discovery of urbanity as an element of culture:

" To try and approach truth on one side after another, not to strive or cry, nor to persist in pressing forward, on any one side, with violence and self-will, — it is only thus, it seems to me, that mortals may hope to catch any vision of that immortal Goddess, whom we shall never see except in outline, but only thus even in outline. He who will do nothing but fight impetuously toward her on his own, one, favourite, particular line, is inevitably destined to run his head into the folds of the black robe in which she is wrapped."

It is very likely from his attempt to put this idea into practice in his own writing that Arnold acquired that peculiar manner of his, which is so offensive to some people and which they qualify as supercilious. He has endeavoured — possibly he has striven a little too perceptibly — to maintain an attitude of ease and detachment, which gives him an air of superiority and condescension to his opponents and which they dislike as much for that reason as anything. He refuses to become too heated, to involve himself too deeply and at the same time to take matters too seriously. He requires of himself a certain disinterestedness in practical concerns which sets him aloof from the rest of the world. The business of criticism is to let alone " all questions of practical consequences and applications "; it " must maintain its independence of the practical spirit and its aims." But right or wrong, this position is evidently an exasperation to practical men, who have no concern for right or wrong as such, particularly when accompanied by Arnold's sarcasm and ridicule of their favourite pursuits. And on this account, as well as by the nature of his ideas themselves, he has inspired a formidable amount of dislike.

To much the same effect — at least another phase of his practical disinterestedness — is his unwillingness to involve himself after the modern fashion in discussions of technique or to confound art with craft. In short, his criticism is essentially an intellectual and moral criticism and it draws its strength from this detachment. As for his borrowings, while it is interesting in illustration of his theory of criticism to trace them to their sources, they amount as loans to little after all. It is not the bare idea, the commonplace that counts; it is the development and above all the application — in his own words, not only " getting to know . . . the best which has been thought and said in the world," but also " through this knowledge turning a stream of fresh and free thought upon our stock notions and habits."

IT would be too much to say that Calderon was ever popular outside of his own country. But once upon a time he did enjoy a kind of exclusive literary vogue or fashion. Seventy-five to a hundred or more years ago in Germany and to some less extent in England and even in France he was an object of interest and mild enthusiasm to the lettered and sophisticated. In England he was happy enough to attract an archbishop, who wrote a little book about him, and to inspire a man of taste to translate or adapt half a dozen of his plays. In America Lowell celebrated his name in verse. Already in Germany, the source of this tepid conflagration, a group of criticasters had been busying themselves with their work of exhumation. Even in France, the country least susceptible to his peculiar appeal, an occasional *littérateur* would condescend to favour him with his notice. I say nothing of Spanish influence upon the earlier drama: that is another subject altogether. But I ought not to omit a reference to the Spanish obligations of a writer so late and so considerable as Grillparzer.

About all this repute there has been something decidedly artificial. Not only were his staunchest admirers so unmeasured as to provoke suspicion and objection; but the interest itself has failed to stand the test of time and cold blood. As a matter of fact it has come to look a good deal like propaganda until it is only as a scholium of German Romanticism that the cult of Calderon appears of much importance. At all events it was to this movement that he owed his revival in the first place. With Shakespeare and Dante he served to form a strong opposition to classicism and to give the Romantic School a consistency which it wanted of itself, and a literary tradition which it pretended to despise but found that it could not do without. It is in this manner that he figures to A. W. Schlegel, who was probably the first to resuscitate his fame, as " der letzte Gipfel der romantischen Poesie " and as the prime representative of the " Religionsgefühl biedrer Heldenmuth, Ehre, und Liebe," which constitutes its groundwork. It is to be supposed that Schlegel was thoroughly familiar with his author; but his remarks on the subject in his " Vorlesungen über dramatische Kunst und Litteratur," which were as much as anything the immediate occasion of the Calderon fad, are more conspicuous for zeal than accuracy.

About Calderon's work, he says, in spite of its quantity " there is nothing random or topsy-turvy: it is all worked out, in masterly fashion, after established and consistent principles, with the most profound artistic intentions. This fact can not be gainsaid, even when the pure and lofty romantico-theatrical style of Calderon is mistaken for mannerism and his daring flights of poetry to the very bounds of the conceivable are regarded as aberrations. In particular he has turned back into matter what his predecessors took for form. [Denn Calderon hat überall das, was seinen Vorgängern schon für Form galt, wieder zum Stoff gemacht.] Nothing less than the noblest and finest flowers satisfied him. Hence it is that he repeats himself in many expressions, images, similitudes — yes, in many a turn of situation [in manchen Spielen der Situationen] for he was too rich else to need borrow from himself, to say nothing of others. The stage-effect [die Erscheinung auf die Bühne] is his first consideration; but this concern, which is with others a limitation, is in his case wholly positive. I know no dramatist who, understanding how to poetize the effect in

such wise, has been at once so sensuous [sinn-
lich kräftig] and so æthereal."

Such is Schlegel's opinion. Like most romantic appreciation it is characteristically vague,
general, and adulatory; above all it has caught
the trick of capitalizing defects and failings.
But such as it is, it was in its time taken up
into criticism and came for a while to constitute the official estimate of the dramatist.
Needless to say, however, it is impossible to
sustain him at such an altitude, though it must
be acknowledged in the next breath that the
romantic position was of itself well taken. In
one respect at least, as I shall try to show, Calderon is no despicable example of the spirit
that he was chosen to illustrate; he is above
all and most exclusively the dramatist of
mood.

It is generally admitted that Calderon is
no delineator of character — and it is the delineation of character that we incline to make
the point of genius nowadays — that on the
whole his interest is less with character than
with action. Indeed, the preference for action
is often referred to as a feature or symptom of
the whole romantic drama, as of romance, including Shakespeare's as well as Calderon's,
in distinction from the classic. And yet Aris-

totle declares explicitly that the mainspring of tragedy is the action. It is evident, then, if the word *action* is to be taken as idiomatic both of romantic and of classic drama, that it must have different meanings in both cases, since a merely superficial comparison shows a wide discrepancy in this particular between the two sorts of plays. The fact is that under the name of action we think more of story, the romance, whereas the Athenian thought of the moral juncture. To our modern minds the essential matter of the action is incident, the moments of which it is composed; to the Greek, the urgency of the occasion. Conformably with our different mental attitudes or habits, we see the action as an affair of interesting elements; he saw it as indivisible emergency. Hence the distinct feelings which the two kinds of action aroused: Shakespeare's, curiosity and suspense; Sophocles', conviction and reassurance. In short, what the Greek saw, was its moral import; the romantic poet, its sensational effect.

Naturally, this difference in the point of view produced a decided difference in the technique or the " art." The romantic dramatist has been tempted to dwell upon his action for its own sake and in detail, to elaborate and draw it out, to lavish his invention and fancy upon it, to complicate and embellish it — in a word, to develop it into a plot or intrigue. In fact, the tendency of his excess, as he has tried to stress his story and yet keep it fit for the stage, has been to make it theatrical rather than dramatic, just as the defect of the Greek was to shrink it into a mere situation without conclusion or issue, as Euripides inclines. To be sure, Shakespeare seldom runs into this extreme; when he drops too far into romance and his plays begin to lose their dramatic virtue, he leaves the stage. But it is Calderon's vice exactly; he is invariably and successfully theatrical.

In so far Schlegel is right: a sense for romance and for the theatrical Calderon has unquestionably. But dearly has he paid for it — at the expense of the dramatic. He is quite lacking in dramatic concentration and development. Even a long play, like Shakespeare's "Macbeth," may have dramatic concentration. But Calderon's plays are unexceptionally diffuse: they spread like water; their movement is centrifugal. Nor has he any particular instinct for development: one thing simply follows another, runs into it fluidly and without consistency; there is no necessity about it of any sort. Like all this Spanish comedia his plays have subjects but no themes; they are tales told in tableaux for those who can not or will not read. That is the worst of a popular drama, or rather stage, that it addresses and must meet just this kind of public. The Elizabethans suffered from the circumstance, though not perhaps so much as the Spaniards. And it is as a result of this sort of determination, at least in part, that Calderon wants reality. His plays are in a manner spectacles and are, almost without exception, morally unconvincing.

Now, a play may have verisimilitude and yet be morally impossible; or on the contrary it may lack verisimilitude and possess moral probability or even inevitability. The latter is peculiarly the case with Shakespeare's "Twelfth Night"; the former with Calderon's "El Mayor Monstruo." It is a matter not merely or solely of action or yet of character, but rather of the relation of the two. Or better, the nature of the action itself is relieved only in its relation with character.

That in Greek tragedy the characters played as such a secondary *rôle* or what we should consider such, is undoubtedly true, and Aristotle is unquestionably right in saying so. Themselves they were more or less representative,

generic rather than individual. And what they
stand for, too, are not so much common types
and species of human beings as the changes and
vicissitudes of human experience. Hence they
serve as a signature or index of the significance
of the action. In the Shakespearean drama,
however, it is the action or at least its issue
which comes to appraise the character; the
character results in the action and is on this
account incapable of evaluating it. He is standing trial himself. But in Spanish, again, not
only is there no gauge at all of the moral import
of the action save and only a story — in Calderon the action neither measures the character
nor is measured by him. It only gives rise to a
succession of passing impressions, whose fluctuations lend the play its idiomatic interest. In
other words, it has no inherent ethical significance — or rather, just as Calderon the playwright turns theatrical, so Calderon the man
turns theological. What little moral sense his
theatre owns is extrinsic and is caught up by
the way in the dialogue, not involved in the
constitution of the play. Juan Valera is quite
right in contending that the Spanish drama is
at all events unmoral if not actually immoral;
though how in the face of such a conclusion he
can maintain its literary pre-eminence is a

wonder to any one who is unfamiliar with the vagaries of romantic criticism.

On the other hand, while the characters in Greek do indeed have this secondary or accessory *rôle* which makes them moral exponents of the action, they still have a distinction and distinctness of their own even while they themselves are strictly coterminous with the drama. Œdipus, Orestes, Antigone are clear enough and discernible through the stream of the action, although unlike Othello, Hamlet, Macbeth, they fail to protrude above its surface and are not, any of them, " characters " in that limited sense in which we sometimes speak of a man to-day as such by force of his standing out conspicuously and in high relief from his surroundings and circumstances — or as the Elizabethan might have said, a " humour." But in the Calderonian drama the characters neither project like Shakespeare's in the manner of the figures in a frieze nor do they resemble, as is the case with Sophocles', a pattern interwoven with the texture of the fabric but always distinguishable from the background; they are, rather, like the shadings of a watered or changeable silk in which the figure is continually losing itself and reappearing more or less uncertainly or elusively like a shadow on the surface of the stuff.

In such a manner do Calderon's characters tend to run into his action and lose any singular identity of their own that it not infrequently seems as though they had been thrown up momentarily by the force of circumstances alone, to fall back upon them and be reabsorbed like bubbles in the stream. Such discriminations are not easy; but it ought to be reasonably clear that this treatment of character is quite different from the Greeks'. And it is conditioned, I believe, by a peculiarity that the critics of Calderon have failed to notice.

To speak as though Calderon had himself but little interest in his people or attention for them and were entirely absorbed by his "fable," is an illegitimate conclusion. All his masks — it would hardly do to call them portraits after what I have been saying, and in fact they are rather masks than portraits — are carefully finished in his own manner. To be sure, great numbers of them bear a strong resemblance to one another — indeed, like his situations they are scarcely distinguishable in themselves, if they are not actually identical. But this effect is mainly due to the way in which the interest is focussed. To speak properly, it is not character as such for which Calderon is concerned except in the subordinate and ancillary fashion, which I have tried to explain, as chips on the current or straws on the wind. It is hardly too much to say that he assumes the character or takes it ready-made; whence his collection of easy types — the man of honour, the gallant, the jealous husband. No, it is not character with which Calderon is preoccupied; it is mood, the transitory and unstable feelings and emotions, the mental fluctuations corresponding with the incidental fluctuations of intrigue and plot.

To this sort of human interest the Greek was hardly awake. It was the steady bearing of character or disposition with which he had to do. His interest was structural. The momentary impression, the shifting play of consciousness, the fits of resolution and infirmity found no echo in his drama. Only occasionally will you find anything like a note of mutability in his tragedy, and that late. As has been so often pointed out his personages go through their work with a single mind and with nothing that can justly be called a vacillation or change of heart. The words, "Τί δῆτα δρῶμεν; μητέρ᾽ ἢ φονεύσομεν," which Euripides puts into the mouth of Orestes at the very instance when his scheme is succeeding and his mother walks into the trap prepared for her, this expression,

" What then to do? Are we to kill our mother? "
is the only example that I can recall of such an
agitation. And while Shakespeare has by no
means ignored mood — while the fascination
of his theatre is due in part to this motive and
the prismatic play of consciousness which it
introduces; yet the moods of his *personæ* have
been deduced from their character and are
regulated and supported by it. " Hamlet " itself,
not to mince matters, is almost exclusively a
study of mood; its significance lies in its sudden alterations and revolutions of temper. But
at the same time all the moods are Hamlet's;
they arise out of his nature and subside upon it
so that finally they compose a characterization
of that protagonist and derive their interest
from that fact. In short Hamlet is, in the jargon
of our day, a temperament.

By comparison, then, we have in Calderon a
dramatist of mood for its own sake. Not that
his moods have no background at all, but that
the background is relatively insignificant. For
the fact is that Calderon's figures are so purely
conventional, so " stock," that the sense of
character virtually vanishes in a wholesale
reading and leaves the perception of mood alone
recognizable. Read any one of his comedias,
" A Secreto Agravio Secreta Venganza " or

" El Médico de su Honra " or even " El Escon-
dido y la Tapada "; and the sense of character
is penetrating enough to a foreigner. They are
all Spaniards of the sixteenth century, infected
with the *pundonor,* the punctilio of their kind;
and in as far as they are neither Anglo-Saxon
nor Nordic nor Anglo-Celtic nor whatever we
like to think ourselves, they appear, taken one
at a time, as sufficiently individual on the
strength of their unfamiliarity. But read all
these plays — or better yet, any half-dozen —
and notice the resemblance, if not the identity
of the essential traits or lineaments, see how
the one person repeats himself again and again,
until you turn your attention from the personality to its affection. In other words, the character remains a constant in every equation;
once admitted, it is negligible and neglected.

Dramatically considered, character is another element than action; hence its development may become detrimental to the drama —
if the play is indeed the thing. Many a strong
character has ruined a good story. Unless the
characters concur with the action — as was the
case with the Greeks', where they swim with it
— they are likely to have a disturbing influence. Their doubts and hesitations, their
scruples and compunctions, may well impede

the course of the drama, their wills resist it. This is one of the causes that Shakespeare's plays or so many of them appear when read to be ill constructed; his characters get in the way. They interfere with his action; not with the course of human events which he mirrors, for the fiction or myth, as distinguished from the play, results from the " oneyeriness " of his characters — but with the dramatic economy they do interfere. Whereas mood, on the contrary, arises directly from the circumstances of the plot; it is the effect of the incidents upon the person concerned. And further, since mood is itself transitory, shifting, unstable, changing with every incident; it naturally will blend with the action, becoming itself a part of the general current. Hence the peculiar shimmering watered appearance of Calderon's fabric, where his *dramatis personæ* seem to run into his action and lose themselves.

On these considerations too it is possible to explain the curious habit of repetition which marks his drama so singularly to a foreigner. Nothing would be easier than to make an extensive list of parallelisms in which the one sentiment recurs again and again in virtually the same words. But then, as I have said, Calderon was not concerned to show an in-

dividuality asserting itself amid the flux of circumstance, but rather the feeling of a pretty
well-defined and limited kind of man, the man
of honour after the Spanish fashion, in a few
representative situations. And since these situations are in the nature of the case recurrent,
their affects and expressions in that one nearly
invariable type will be recurrent too. Not that
every capital situation in Calderon is identical
with every other, though there is a likeness
among them all. But it is hardly too much to
say that the foundation of the Calderonian
Comedia is formed by a small set of stock
situations.

> " ¿ Es comedia de Don Pedro
> Calderon, donde ha de haber
> Por fuerza amante escondido
> O rebozada mujer? "

There is always the lover, frequently surprised
by the husband who, unlike the French *mari*,
is usually the heroic and sympathetic person-
age, under more or less compromising circumstances for which it behooves him to exact ven-
geance for the satisfaction of his honour. But
the skill with which these commonplaces are
varied so that a little shading is introduced
into the collection, is remarkable, it must be

granted. And as the minute ingredients of the same old salad change a little, the emotional responses of the characters, in the technical sense of the word, change also, even while the language remains much the same, in a manner easy enough to appreciate though not very easy to define. There is in this wise an undeniable subtlety in Calderon's drama, which the cursory or partial spectator might fail to notice. But on this score we who are of the Shakespearean tradition can hardly afford to throw stones. And I suppose that the observation is true of any great literature after its kind, that it carries two messages — one obvious and superficial, the other difficult and recondite.

And so while the Spanish comedia has no great sense for the thematic either in character or plot, its sensibility to mood and its expression does result in the creation or realization of a certain kind and number of situations — mood-situations, perhaps I may call them to mark their affiliation with the affections of the *dramatis personæ* and their distinction from anything constitutional or organic. As such they may be described as a kind of convulsion, a sort of spasm affecting action, as mood is to be viewed as a kind of spasm affecting personality. In other words the Spanish action is as temperamental as the Spanish character and equally excitable. Or is it the other way around? Was it this taste for pointedness of incident which developed the *penchant* for mood as its best means of exhibition?

At all events it is a fretful drama. And the impression is not a little enhanced by the verse in which it is written. To the English reader it seems quite impossible that what is virtually a ballad measure should ever be susceptible of tragedy. Certainly it lacks solemnity. And besides, it wants the long dramatic crescendo to which we are accustomed in English and Greek, and in French as well — in short, in the languages on which we have formed our taste. But it served the purposes of the Spanish theatre nevertheless. In spite of the fact that eloquence and majesty are impossible to it, there is a kind of rough and ready poetry about it, such as we have brought ourselves to admire in Percy. It is not epigrammatic but it is capable of making a point — it lends itself to the quip or quibble, the sort of theatrical casuistry to which the Spanish were addicted: —

> " Y así vengo, cuando yace
> En el supulcro del sueño
> Toda mi casa cadáver ";

or better, perhaps — at least more in the Shake-spearean vein, though without its impressive-ness : —

> " ! Qué mal hice quando necio
> De amor, y de su violencia,
> Culpé á Antonio que adorase
> A aquella gitana, á aquella
> Que en los teatros del mundo
> Hizo la mayor tragedia ! "

I have been speaking of Calderon very much as though it were all a matter of tragedy or serious drama exclusively. Such, however, is not the case. And yet the great illustration of Spanish comedy, of course, is Cervantes, not Calderon. Even as a playwright Calderon is inferior to Lope de Vega. On the whole, " El Alcalde de Zalamea " would be considered, I suppose, Calderon's best piece. In point of fact it belongs to Lope de Vega. There is nothing, at least there never has been anything against one dramatist's appropriating another's sub-ject. But in this case the *procédé*, the facture of " El Alcalde " is not Calderon's ; he has not made the play his own — it is quite anoma-lous and of another technique. And in comedy Lope's superiority becomes particularly evi-dent. His " El Perro del Hortelano " is the most entertaining play of the period that I have read in the language. It is not so very unlike Marivaux somehow; for instance "Les Fausses Confidences." Nor is "Los Melindres de Belisa" without a good dramatic core. The difficulty lies in what we should esteem the curious dramatic irrelevances with which the plays are developed. Their faults are those which I have just been discussing — extravagance, lack of verisimilitude, moral improbability, and in this case a misconception of the properly comic and a preference for the accidental and coincidental, for misapprehension and *contretemps* — to say nothing of the diffuseness which comports so ill with the charter of drama.

For these reasons among many Cervantes is the Spaniard who ministers most agreeably to our sense of comedy, that sort of comedy which is so saturated with humour as to be hardly distinguishable from it. For this *genre,* if it may be so called, narrative is in itself a much better medium than drama; it is ampler and much less constrained, and is capable of broader effects. To be sure, there is a great deal to be overcome in "Don Quijote." As a burlesque of the chivalric we can only make the best of it. And no doubt, too, Cervantes' fun is often pretty rough and obstreperous for a twentieth century stomach wonted to the titillations of innuendo and insinuation. Nothing ages so rapidly as the fashion of mirth, and the jest that tickled the father may nauseate the son. The eternal heckling to which the Don is mercilessly exposed for two thousand pages or so but works its own reaction. Naturally these seemingly interminable wastes of buffoonery and horseplay and slapstick have their oases. I would mention only the gathering at the *venta,* with the tales of the Cautivo and the Curioso Impertinente. About this episode in particular there is at least something like poetic verity; it builds up in the imagination into a sort of illusion which persists in recollection — I had almost said like a situation of Dickens', different as the two humorists are. But it is only a respite after all. The public must have been stupider in those days, if that is possible. At least their density was greater than is ours — their molecular constitution more stable, so that it took more to dissolve them into tears or laughter; or it may be that they could bear more laughing and crying without the mood's disintegrating. At all events the effort which Cervantes has expended upon his effect has turned out to be an embarrassment. And to add to our difficulties, the story itself is of the old picaresque or perambulatory type. A marvellous achievement for the age — it antedates "Tom Jones" by a century and a half — it marks nevertheless a relatively rudimentary stage in the history of the art so called of prose fiction.

But after all, while I do not belittle these failings, which the Romanticists in their habitual fashion were quick to capitalize, still Cervantes' humour in any case runs very much deeper. There is about it a large and luminous tolerance, a profound humanity — not the humanity which is blind to human foible and vanity and vice, the silly official optimism of the professional humanitarian, which blinks the fact of evil and misery and error — or even, I doubt, that "touch of nature which makes the whole world kin" in a universal frailty. But to be disabused of the deception, without losing interest in the reality, of life; to suspect that very reality, perhaps, and yet to retain sufficient indulgence to expatiate at large upon the momentous trivialities of human experience — this is in itself a triumph of good humour. Above all, it is Cervantes' ability to recognize the portion of illusion in the nobility and elevation of man and of his civilization which

makes of the juxtaposition of Don Quijote and
Sancho Panza an enduring symbol of its kind.
He is not a myth-maker like Plato; but in his
amused appreciation of the contrast between
his two characters, the visionary and the pragmatic, in particular their lien upon one another and its fabulous source, I seem to see a
gloss on Plato's economy of the gold, the silver,
and the bronze men. And so it is that in his wide
and at times otiose elaboration of his theme he
has won a position as one of the three or four
great representatives of the humorous comedy of life, with Aristophanes and Shakespeare,
far and away above his dramatic compatriots.

And yet, in conclusion, this drama itself, so
negligent on the whole of theme and character,
has endowed modern literature with one of its
perennial motives and one of its immortal characters. For the latter service the credit belongs
to Tirso de Molina with his " Burlado de
Sevilla y Convidado de Piedra," the original of
Don Juan. For the former Calderon's " La
Vida es Sueño " is immediately responsible.
The sentiment is, of course, a commonplace;
but to Calderon's development, I think, it may
be said to owe in large part its currency — in
fact, that very familiarity which makes it a
commonplace:

" ¿ Que es la vida? Un frenesi.
¿ Que es la vida? Una illusion,
Una sombra, una faccion,
Y el mayor bien es pequeño:
Que toda la vida es sueño,
Y los sueños sueño son."

Such are the unexpectednesses of genius.

MONTAIGNE

"ON a tout dit sur Montaigne," says Sainte-Beuve, "depuis plus de deux siècles qu'on en parle " — or if we take the publication of the " Essais " in 1580 as the point of departure, nearly three and a half centuries by this time. Very likely. The point is that in the courses of the whirligig we like to call progress the work of Montaigne is constantly to be done over; and in default of a writer of his competence and complaisance there is little or nothing to do but refer again and again to what he has in so many respects done so admirably already. I mean, to sketch the vision of life and the world that appears recurrently to the eye of the disinterested by-stander — the man of detachment, speculative, skeptical, and curious — sufficiently withdrawn from the activities and ambitions of his fellows to be untroubled and undazzled by them — disenchanted and sophisticated. In its way such a performance is meat for the moralist. It is a work of intelligence, not of science either social or political. That it involves an element of personal illusion, can not be helped; we are all of us who are our own masters, the slaves of our dispositions still. But it is not wholly singular on that account. For just as there are ages of faith and of question, periods of expansion and of contraction, and between them intervals of indifference and apathy, perhaps of *recueillement* and recollection, when it seems as though the exertions of the human spirit had at last exhausted its capacity for convictions of any kind; so in every age or period there are minds of such a sort, neither Gladstones nor Huxleys, which will not compose with the forces of the time; and of these Montaigne still remains the spokesman as he has done ever since he first opened his mouth. To be sure, the world has spun a little since the close of the sixteenth century. Our knowledge of physical nature alone has become so particular as to affect our conception of man's position and status in detail. But all this agitation has served merely to encourage the superstition of the modern man and confirm the cynicism of the onlooker. How long is it since we have had a serious moralist of any scope? And while Montaigne is not highly serious in all his ways, yet that very fact makes him only the more acceptable mouthpiece of this third party, which is itself, perhaps, somewhat to seek in the article of high seriousness, being officially neither one thing nor the other.

Michel Eyquem de Montaigne, of the Order of Saint Michel, was born at Montaigne in Perigord on February 28, 1533. Of a family of merchants, he was trained to the law and served as Counsellor to the Parliament of Bordeaux. At the age of thirty-seven he retired to a life of leisure on his estate. Thereafter he travelled a little in Germany and Italy, and was twice elected mayor of Bordeaux. But on the whole he devoted himself pretty exclusively to his rather desultory reading and musing without much concern for the bickering of factions and the *fronderie* of the time. The first edition of the "Essays," the result of ten years' rumination, appeared in 1580 in two books. In 1588 it was superseded by a version containing a third book quite new as well as copious additions to the two preceding books mostly in the way of quotation and allusion. A third rendering, the edition of Mademoiselle Gournay, his spiritual foster-daughter, was issued in 1595 and embodied all the author's addenda, marginalia, errata — a hodge-podge and patchwork of editorship. On the whole, the handiest and best modern edition for the general reader is that of

Motheau and Jouaust (Librarie des Biblio-
philes) which preserves the text of 1588 intact
and subjoins the interpolations of 1595 in foot-
notes. As for English translations, a sort of
work that has so often proved delightful to the
amateur however exceptionable it may appear
to the scholar, Florio's rendering is an inimitable specimen of Elizabethanism; while
Charles Cotton's, dating from the second half
of the eighteenth century, is commended by
Edward Dowden as a masterpiece.

According to Montaigne's verbal portrait
of himself, and he was a dabster at self-
portraiture, he had a " *taille forte et ramassée,*"
a bold, intrepid nose, a high and narrow fore-
head deeply sutured, a sparse sixteenth-century
beard and moustache. Of no great figure or
height he must have appeared rather trifling,
a slight fellow physically, beside such men of
their hands as Henry of Navarre. But his constitution, he protests, was vigorous; and in
spite of the stone, which he had " inherited "
from his father, he declares himself never so
happy as when on horseback, " *où sont mes
plus larges entretiens.*" Further, a quiet and
retiring country-gentleman with a wife and six
daughters; a great traveller of sedentary habit;
a fancier of the ladies with a taste for privacy

and seclusion; an ardent friend and a cautious
trimmer; an admirer of pagan virtue and the
wisdom of the ancients; a gentle voluptuary
with a stoical turn of mind; a child of the
Renaissance and a son of the Church, a devout
Roman Catholic — such, as recorded by himself, are the principal lineaments and markings
of this "*être ondoyant et divers.*"

His "essays" are usually brief, more or less
patchworky — "vagabond," he calls them —
personal, "intimate," egoistic, and yet — what
word shall I use? humane? proper to his kind?
humankindly? They are all self-conscious, his
own responses, as it were, to the observations of
his authors, and are larded with quotations and
references accordingly. His phraseology is extremely happy — pointed, picturesque, unexpected, but homely and idiomatic, often to the
modern ear with an effect of colloquialism, like
the familiar speech of our grandfathers — or
grandmothers.

His *pièce de résistance* — I should not say
his masterpiece or his show-piece; that is probably "Upon Some Verses of Virgil" — is the
"Apology of Raimond Sebond." It is much
more comprehensive than the usual run of his
work, and far more carefully composed. Above
all, it is the best or handiest key to his mind —

an admirable example of his characteristic
irony or *malice*. Bustling to the defense of his
author's natural theology, a sort of sixteenth
century deism, he proposes ingenuously to de-
molish the two main engines which have been
raised against it by its enemies, the conservative and the reactionary.

And to begin with he observes that the attack
turns in principle on the fact that Sebond's is a
work of the reason; and as far as Christianity is
concerned, it at least is incapable of rational
justification: it is divine, and the divine is
appreciable by faith alone. In reply to the exception Montaigne points out that Christianity, as it manifests itself in humanity, shows
no sign of celestial origin or sanction. If our
religion were actually divine, he exclaims, how
very different we who profess it should be from
what we in fact are! But as matters stand Christianity is patently in the same case with the
other religions and may justly be treated in the
same manner — rationally.

So much for the first bout. But mark the
" apologist's " duplicity. Either Sebond, and his
theology with him, are reduced to an *absurdum*
by the powers of sarcasm in virtue of the over-
whelming authority of Christianity, for who
would be so mad as to impeach the sanctity of

the Church? Or else Sebond is justified of his
rationalism but at the expense of the primacy
of the Christian religion. Of the two, which?
Does the "Apology" cloak an ironical attack
upon Sebond or a covert insinuation against
Catholicism? Or neither? Is it merely one of
those *jeu d'esprit* or playful exercises of the intellect with which a flippant skepticism delights
to amuse itself? Or is it one of those familiar-
ities which the devout sometimes allow themselves on the strength of their devotion?

But again, in the weakness of Sebond's
"natural evidences" Montaigne recognizes the
second of his author's liabilities. This is a leak
that he cannot stop; he can only seek to disguise its gravity. Weak let us grant them then;
but what do you expect? They are the strongest
available to the unassisted intelligence. Strip
a man of faith and his supernatural credentials,
and what can he produce in proof of his own
paramount and central position in the scheme
of salvation? Why, he is no better, rationally
considered, than the beasts that perish, — may-
be, a little worse, after the moral of Pyrrho.

Here, then, is the second line of "defense."
Taken ingenuously and as a sequel to the preceding, the argument, in finally disabling reason as the instrument of truth, would appear to

depose man from the primacy of creation by undermining the rational foundation on which it had just been left dependent. Another absurdity? Or is it quite so simple after all? Granted that at first Sebond has been justified of his confidence in the religious application of the reason, what exactly is the case in the end? Does Christianity finally fall with him? But on the other hand, if Christianity has been slyly circumvented in the previous skirmish, what is left of it now that argument fails it? Complete bankruptcy? Or blind credulity? What is the difference? Is Montaigne a skeptic of faith or of reason? And are we in reality as in appearance confronted with an ironical " apology " — an apology not of Sebond but of the Church? Lanson declares that " the sense of all these fine speeches [*ces beaux discours*] is an absolute condemnation of this theologian's (Sebond's) design and in detail the peculiar defender (Montaigne) gives his client the lie at every instant [*donne à chaque moment des dementis à son client*]." But Miss Norton, who has spoken on this subject with authority, takes the " Apology " in good faith and at the foot of the letter, remarking that " Montaigne does not perceive that this conclusion is fatal to Sebond's book." But is he quite so naïf, this Montaigne?

As for me — he carries his tongue in his cheek
too habitually that his artless little stutters and
stammers should dispel the suspicions that I
conceive of him from time to time.

But at all events, whether consciously or not,
whatever may have been his intentions, or
whether he was only amusing himself, though
that is vice enow — he did at least discover the
method of Christian apologetics which was to
prevail for the next century or so — namely,
the disgrace of reason and the glorification of
faith, the subornation of the human heart. It
is the way that Pascal followed — only he goes
on from the point where Montaigne rests.
" Tout notre raisonnement se réduit à céder au
sentiment." Why has the church always been so
fearful of the intelligence? " Naturellement
même cela vous fera croire et vous abêtira."
Admitted that the heart has its reasons which
reason knows nothing of; but so has the head
its reasons too. And in view of the contribu-
tions of St. Paul and Plato such denigration
seems as unwise as ungrateful.

Naturally — or should I say, inevitably? —
Montaigne every now and then has the misfor-
tune to overreach himself. It is so difficult to be
clever without being too clever. Perhaps it is
hardly too much to say that his whole enter-

prise is a little extravagant, so much of the success of irony depends upon a prudent mediocrity — at least a kind of provocative coyness, and Montaigne's muse is not always so demure as she ought to be. The pretension, for instance, that human intelligence is at a practical disadvantage in comparison with animal insensibility, that it is, if anything, a source of moral inferiority and infirmity — seriously, such claims, and they are much in fashion to-day, are either impudent or imbecile.

"The philosopher Pyrrho, exposed to the danger of a storm at sea, did but advise those with him to imitate the resolution and serenity of a pig that had been brought along and was watching the tempest without terror and without alarm."

This is Pascal's line — to a point; but it is there that Pascal's nature, in spite of his penitential humour, comes into its own: —

"Man is but a reed . . . but a reed that thinks. It needs not that the whole universe should take up arms to crush him; a fume, a drop of water is enough to kill him. But when the world has crushed him, he is nobler still

than his assassin for he knows that he dies and
the advantage that nature has of him she knows
it not."

But either way, whether inadvertent or not,
these occasional *bêtises* of Montaigne's are sus-
picious, on the part of one professing the theo-
retic life, of a lack of intellectual conscience, of
good faith. They are comparable in their way
with certain petulances of Renan's. For it is
clear, whatever the impression produced by the
" Apology " as such, that Montaigne is im-
proving the occasion to express a number of
ideas that have been gathering in his head for
a great while, detachments from the main body
of his philosophy. Philosophy? Speculation —
Weltanschauung is what I mean, but unfortunately there is no English equivalent — or
French for the matter of that — philosophy has
always served our turn without undue ambiguity. Well, this philosophy of Montaigne's,
as far as it may be gleaned from those pages, is
just the philosophy to wink at such an infidelity
now and then, a philosophy of easy virtue. The
world is an illusion; or rather, it is the ground,
the screen of any number of possible illusions,
one of which is quite as good as another, so that
it is the part of wisdom to take none of them

very seriously but to flirt with any or all of them impartially turn and turn about.

"Maintes-fois (comme il m'advient de faire volontiers) ayant pris pour exercise et pour esbat à maintenir une contraire opinion à la mienne, mon esprit, s'applicant et tournant de ce costé-là, m'y attache si bien que je ne trouve plus la raison de mon premier jugement, et m'en depars. Je m'entraine quasi où je penche, comment que ce soit, et m'emporte de mon propre pois."¹

Of reality we have no certain knowledge; we can not trust the evidence of our senses, to say nothing of guarding against hallucinations. Our reason, " c'est un instrument de plomb et de cire, alongeable, ployable et accommodable à

---

¹ The fact is, it is impossible to translate Montaigne, as impossible as it is to translate a poet. For those of another day — and of another tongue — his language is fully half his fascination. For that reason I prefer as a rule Florio's version to Cotton's — on account of the opalescence of the medium. Nevertheless, in spite of the absolute inadequacy of both I subjoin now and then out of curiosity an example of one or the other; for instance:

" Many times (as commonly it is my hap to doe) having for exercise and sport-sake undertaken to maintaine an opinion contrarie to mine, my mind applying and turning it selfe that way, doth so tie me unto it as I finde no more the reason of my former conceit, and so I leave it. Where I encline, there I entertain my selfe, how soever it be, and am carried away by mine owne weight." — Florio

tous biais et à toutes mesures." [2] At best the world is but an " arrangement," an ideal construction, a predicate of the self. Who has the grammar creates the illusion — the poet, the lawgiver, the orator, the theologian. " J'appelle tous-jours raison cette apparence de discours que chacun forge en soy; cette raison de la condition de laquelle il y en peut avoir cent contraires autour d'un mesme subject . . . il ne reste que la suffisance de la sçavoir contourner." [3] As for the rank and file, they adopt the particular formula they find prevailing, " le jargon communement tenu, avec tout son bastiment et attelage d'argumens et de preuves." And so " se remplit le monde and se confit en fadesse et en mensonge." And worse still, not only is human faculty incompetent in itself, it is so occluded by these inventions and circumventions that it is insensible of what has no current name or etiquette and of other aspects than those so labelled and memorial-

[2] " It is an instrument of lead and wax, stretching, pliable, and that may be fitted to all byases, and squared to all measures."
— Florio

[3] " I alwaies call reason, that apparance or shew of discourses, which every one deviseth or forgeth in himselfe: that reason, of whose condition, there may be a hundred, one contrary to another, about one selfe same subject . . . there remaines nothing but the skill and sufficiency to know how to turne and winde the same."
— Florio

ized. " Et j'en laisse plus librement aller mes caprices en public; d'autant que, bien qu'ils soyent nez chez moy et sans example, je sçay qu'ils trouveront leur conformité et relation à quelque humeur ancienne; et ne faudra quelqu'un de dire: 'Voyla d'ou il le print!' " [4]

Impossible as it is ever to know, it is possible, however, to go on forever inquiring. Truth may be unsearchable and past finding out, for how should we recognize her even if we did happen to meet her. But opinion is inexhaustible as long as

> " age to age succeeds
> Blowing a noise of tongues and deeds,
> A dust of systems and of creeds,"

and provides an endless matter of speculation and entertainment. It is not the quarry but the chase, not the port but the voyage; to be drifting timelessly on " cette mer vaste, trouble et ondoyante des opinions humaines," that is the beatitude. The mind of man — not the " phenomena of the universe," as Huxley grandilo-

---

[4] " And therefore doe I suffer my humours or caprices more freely to pass in publike; Forasmuch as though they are borne with, and of me, and without any patterne; well I wot, they will be found to have relation to some ancient humour, and some shall be found, that will both know and tell whence, and of whom I have borrowed them." — Florio

quently says, nor the providence of God — not
Nature nor Divinity, but the thoughts of man,
" cet être divers et ondoyant " is the legitimate
subject of philosophic meditation and won-
derment.

And here, it is not improbable, we touch the
nerve of our particular philosopher — that personal preference or taste, that set of involuntary attractions and repulsions to which every
body of thought, the more so the more loose-
jointed it is, responds reflexively. He does not
doubt, as he represents his Pyrrho doing, for
the sake of doubting, but for the sake of using
his wits. His skepticism is a secondary characteristic. You may say that speculation is naturally unsettling; but still more does self-
conscious speculation shrink from taking its
own life. Were certainty easy of access, the
game, this interminable patience, would soon
be over. But Montaigne has removed the term
and has set the farthest reach of wisdom in the
realization of that ignorance which comes of an
insatiable curiosity. Learning is a by-product,
and if anything, to be deplored — or at least
worn with humility like other great material
possessions, wealth or popularity or even virtue
— as children play not for the sake of health
but for the fun of it. " Les livres m'ont servi

non tant d'instruction que d'exercitation." Not even ignorance is an end; it is a condition. In this respect he classifies the genus man into three species: — those who are naïvely and innocently ignorant; those who are wise in their own conceit and pride themselves upon their little learning; and those who have convinced themselves of their own ignorance. The first is far and away superior to the second, the ignoramus to the pedant. But the third alone, like Socrates, is wise — not in his knowledge but in his state — obviously, since the sole difference between the first and the third, the virgin consciousness and the convertite, lies not in any positive acquisition but rather in a change of heart, a conviction of the mortal sin of intellectual vanity.

Exactly what is the character of this conversion Montaigne does not explain. Its instrument appears to consist of a kind of dialectic in which the penitent or patient reader questions and answers himself of his author. "Que sçay-je?" But the result is not knowledge but experience, an immediate acquaintance with one's self and its capabilities. "Fay ton faict et te congnoy." The difficulty is that as usual he is reluctant to arrive; he has a horror of attainment, of the *fini* and the *tranché*. And he argues

at large of the soul's ultimate inability to attain
to a knowledge of its own nature. As a result
one's possibility is but an infirmity. In this way
we come to know ourselves in a negative or
nihilistic fashion, which makes of doubt a question, as well as of certainty, and offers another
opportunity of mental activity, not to say of
moral ambiguity after the manner of the
" Apology." The virtue of course is in the in-
quisition; " car encore faut il quelque degré
d'intelligence à pourvoir remarquer qu'on
ignore et faut pousser à une porte pour sçavoir
qu'elle nous est close." [5]

Practically, however, to spend one's life
pushing at every door is out of the question;
the practice of a thorough-going skepticism, no
matter how exhilarating it may be, is quite impossible. It is necessary to effect some sort of
compromise, to strike up a concordat with the
world. And in so doing he deserts almost insensibly the ranks of the Skeptics and arranges to
carry on the business of life more or less com-
modiously in the shelter of the Porch. The advantage of knowing oneself as far as it goes
consists in distinguishing that self from other

---

[5] " — for a certain degree of intelligence is required to be
able to know that a man knows not: and we must push against
a door to know whether it be bolted against us or no." — Cotton

things, "the skin from the shirt." The matters that are of us, that appertain and are of our competence (τὰ ἐφ' ἡμῖν) subject, I presume, to a kind of pragmatic test, as which will come off and which will not — these matters are comparatively few, but they are, in our ignorance of ends, all that matter. We are liable to accident; we can not tell what the next four and twenty hours will bring forth. To-day we are in health, prosperous and surrounded by friends and flatterers; to-morrow, like as not, we shall be stripped and striped. Grandeur, honour, the gauds of ambition slip through our fingers.

> "The glories of our blood and state
> Are shadows, not substantial things."

In this emergency it is desirable, since the stars confound our arithmetic, that we should put ourselves out of reach of disaster by confining our solicitude to our own commandment. "Ne pouvant reigler les evenemens, je me reigle moy-mesme, et m'applique à eux, s'ils ne s'appliquent à moy." By all means let us keep our money on call. "Il faut avoir femmes, enfans, biens, et sur tout de la santé, qui peut; mais non pas s'attacher en maniere que tout nostre heur en depende: il se faut reserver une arriereboutique toute nostre, toute franche, en laquelle nous establissons nostre vraye liberté et principale retraicte et solitude." [6] Epictetus, of course; but then wisdom was not born with us. Our wills are our own, Montaigne seems convinced; to be sure, they may be attainted — but only of treason. In short, his practical wisdom, his art of living in the world with resignation, if not with pleasure, the condition of this pensive tenancy of the backshop issues in the inculcation of self-control, a volitional delimitation of the self corresponding to the cognitional, to use our own rather sophomoric " jargon," " La vraye liberté, c'est pouvoir toutes choses sur soy." Such is the theme and substance of his last book, published eight years later than the others, his final utterance and presumably his maturest.

For all its cynicism his askesis is not identical, it is to be noticed, with the *Jenseitigkeit* of the ascetic who by an effort of mortification has ceased to live already and who dreads nothing further since nothing worse can happen to him

[6] " Wives, children, and goods must be had, and especially health by him that can get it; but we are not so to set our hearts upon them that our happiness must have its dependence upon them; we must reserve a backshop, wholly our own and entirely free, wherein to settle our true liberty, our principal solitude and retreat." — Cotton

now that the amputation is over. " Il n'y a rien de mal en la vie pour celuy qui a bien comprins que la privation de la vie n'est pas mal." With this sort of discipline Montaigne shows no great sympathy. In spite of his stoical *velléités* there are too many Epicurean components in his make-up — the heritage, perhaps, of the Renaissance. He is free, for example, of the symptomatic stoic melancholy, the dreary resignation — one would not be far out in calling it the resignation of despair of a world where all things are for the best, the *amor fati,* the *s'abêtir* of stoicism. To be sure, he has his moments of depression; he is inclined to be out of conceit with these little writings of his; and anon he has a sigh for his increasing years and the plight of his country. His whole philosophy too, it must be conceded, — and the observation is true of the stoic way in general which was a kind of worldliness after all *au rebours,* a means of getting on with the world as it is by acquiescing in it — the sum of his sagacity is in the nature of a preparation for the worst; it is a tacit recognition of the human extremity. " A faute d'avoir assez de fermeté pour soufrir l'importunité des accidens contraires ausquels nous sommes subjects et pour ne me pouvoir tenir tendu à regler et ordonner les affaires, je nourris

autant que je puis en moy cett' opinion, m'aban-
donnant du tout à la fortune, de prendre toutes
choses au pis, et ce pis là, me resoudre à le
porter doucement et patiemment." [7] But it has
at least one superiority over its original — over
the profession of Marcus Aurelius and the
modern confessors — it refuses to becloud the
moral issue by juggling with the reality of evil.
" Observe what death is," says Marcus Aurelius, " and that if a man looks at it in itself
and by the analytic power of reflection dissolves
all his imagings, he will find it to be nothing but
a work of nature; and if any one is afraid of a
work of nature, he is a child." " The child in the
soul that fears death," Plato said before him.
But the dread of death is something more than
an error of mind. Death is an evil, and a very
real and shocking one if we are to credit St.
Paul's *sous-entendres*. And Montaigne's evils
are real evils too, not painted devils. They are
something to be avoided if possible; if not, to
be endured with obstinacy — not to be shuffled

[7] " For want of constancy enough to support the shock of
adverse accidents to which we are subject, and of patience seriously to apply myself to the management of my affairs, I nourish
as much as I can this in myself, wholly leaving all to fortune,
' to take all things at the worst, and to resolve to bear that worst
with temper and patience.' "

So Cotton; he bungles the shading, and Florio does too: as
I said to begin with, Montaigne can not be translated.

away under the disguise of blessings. When the plague broke out in Bordeaux during his mayoralty he wrote excusing himself from attendance in the city for the continuance of the epidemic. But of the last sickness of his friend Étienne de la Boétie he says: —

"Il me dit alors que sa maladie estoit un peu contagieuse, et, outre cela, qu'elle etoit mal-plaisante et melancolique; qu'il cognoissoit tresbien mon naturel, et me prioit de n'estre avec lui que par boutées, mais le plus souvent que je pourrois. Je ne l'abandonnay plus." [8]

But notwithstanding his pessimism, his rejection of the lie in stoicism, his humour is cheerful, even merry for all his momentary *défaillances*. In his essay, "De la Tristesse," he remarks, "Je suis le plus exempt de cette passion." In particular he is exempt from that peculiar harrassment of spirit which has cursed a later generation of unbelief, though it is his skepticism, I suppose, that has recommended him to the modern world: he has no strain of

[8] "He told me then that his disease [the pest] was rather contagious, and besides, that it was disagreeable and depressing; that he undertood my disposition and begged me to be with him only by spells but as often as I could. — I never left him again."

the romantic nostalgia in him. He has moods
but no moodiness. He prides himself on having
lived on the whole a happy life. " Je ne fay rien
sans gayeté." On this score he challenges comparison with Pascal. In essentials their philoso-
phies are as like as two peas. They both reject
the authority of reason and retain the authority of faith. But with what alacrity Montaigne
throws himself upon the discards; with what
glee he sorts and combines them; what entertainment he finds in playing these factitious
hands like an interminable solitaire — child's
play, perhaps, but instructive too, he seems to
think, of chance and probability. " Je n'ayme,
pour moy, que des livres ou plaisans et faciles
qui me chatouillent, ou ceux qui me consolent
et conseillent à regler ma vie et ma mort." [9]
As a matter of fact he seldom read longer than
an hour at a time. " Les difficultez si j'en ren-
contre en lisant, je n'en ronge pas mes ongles;
je les laisse là après leur avoir faire une charge
ou deux." [10] And consistently he has a tenderness for Plutarch and Seneca because " la

[9] " As for my selfe, I love no books, but such as are pleasant
and easie, and which tickle me, or such as comfort and counsell
me, to direct my life and death." — Florio

[10] " I do not bite my nails about the difficulties I meet with
in my reading; after a charge or two, I give them over."
— Cotton

science que j'y cherche, elle y est traictée à
pieces et décousues." [11] Poetry he places among
the books " simplement plaisans." Virgil, Lu-
cretius, Catullus, and Horace take precedence.
" Virgil's Georgics j'estime le plus plein et ac-
comply ouvrage de poesie." At Greek, however,
he shies. " Je ne me prens guiere . . . aux
grecs, parce que mon jugement ne se satisfaict
pas d'une moyenne intelligence," having never
mastered the language. Plutarch, he says, he
read in French. There is a story about an
" Odyssey " of his, but it is probably a myth.
No doubt he felt something antipathetic in
the language or its writers. His taste is all for
Latin. He prefers a secondary tradition, a dis-
tillate, such as he was capable of making himself. At the same time he does not take to the
moderns (nouveaux) either, " pour ce que les
anciens me semblent plus tendus et plus
roides." Perhaps it was the Roman port, the
Roman *morgue* that tickled his fancy: he appears to esteem the Spartan spirit above the
Athenian; his hero is the Cornelean. For Dante
he has not much to say, though he quotes him

[11] " Both have this excellent commodity for my humour, that
the knowledge I seek in them, is there so scatteringly and loosely
handled, that whosoever readeth them is not tied to plod long
upon them." — Florio

now and then. Within his limits he discrimi-
nates as a rule very shrewdly; but his bounds
are arbitrary and not infrequently whimsical.
He is reluctant to credit that Terence wrote
the plays ascribed to him because of a prejudice against his station. His criticism is im-
pressionistic; his essay "Of Books" antici-
pates the kind of thing for which we have come
to reserve the name appreciation wherein "personality" is supposed to do the work of principle and whereof the following passage might
serve as a formula: — " Je dy librement mon
advis de toutes choses, voire et de celles qui
surpassent à l'adventure ma suffisance, et que
je ne tiens aucunement estre de ma jurisdiction: ce que j'en opine, ce n'est pas aussi pour
establir la grandeur et mesure des choses, mais
pour faire connoistre la mesure et force de ma
veue." [12]

For principles as such, it is fairly evident by
this time, Montaigne had little use. Maxims,
aphorisms, adages, to such homely summaries
of human experience he lent a not unwilling
ear; his own reliance he put upon the supple

[12] " I speak my opinion freely of all things, even of those
that, perhaps exceed my capacity, and that I do not conceive to
be, in any wise, under my jurisdiction. And, accordingly, the
judgment I deliver, is to show the measure of my own sight, and
not of the things I make so bold to criticise." — Cotton

descriptive phrase. Of a science of history he is incredulous, generalization is so invariably at odds with reality. If there is one thing of which he is thoroughly intolerant it is the man of habit. "La vie est un mouvement inegal, irregulier, et multiforme." Its law is fluctuation; and assurance is to be found, if at all, in versatility; immobility is fatal, as the rope-walker depends upon agility not obduracy. For his own part he associates by contrast and is an adept in the practice of the *volte-face*. He is as ingenious at one time in his praise of folly as he is at another in his commendation of wisdom. But somehow or other in his dizzy revolutions he always contrives a return upon himself and his own centre of gravity — always in unstable equilibrium and yet never quite losing his balance, successful though he may be in turning the heads of the spectators.

And so I come out very nearly by "the same door where in I went." In view of all these considerations, particularly of this cast and habit of spirit, can it be that Montaigne is really as serious as he pretends to be, or possibly thinks he is, in exempting faith from the disabilities of reason? Does not the infirmity of the mind affect belief as well as its other faculties and argue nothing more reliable than credulity?

But if Montaigne were merely paying lip-
service to the truth and certainty of revelation
and the infallibility of the church as its depositary and expounder, he was certainly taken
seriously; and that is the point after all, that
he could make such a profession anyway with a
straight face in the teeth of his own skepticism
— this compartmenting of consciousness as a
matter of course being at least a curious trait
of the man and of his time, an effect and consequence in part of the Renaissance.

As far as I can make anything of that period
of pregnant confusion, the Renaissance had at
this stage developed three characteristic activities or interests — erudition, virtuosity, and
humanism. The Scaligers and Benvenuto Cellini will serve respectively to illustrate the first
two. The last is represented by Erasmus and
— Montaigne, better by Montaigne, I believe,
than by Erasmus, at least more interestingly.
Montaigne's humanism is very nearly, if not
quite, uncontaminated by artistic *velléités;*
and if it has a tincture of pedantry, the dose is
strictly measured; his element exists all but
pure and isolated. And yet in one sense my nomenclature is faulty for the reason that each of
these interests was as a rule pursued with such
exclusiveness as to become an engrossment or

species of virtuosity in itself. In any case their
peculiarity lies in their indifference to all practical and ethical concerns. They have no public
or religious anxieties beyond keeping on the
right side of the temporal and spiritual powers.
Think of Cellini, robber, ravisher, assassin —
blasphemous, impious, sacrilegious — but a
zealous artist. Even Erasmus shows traces of
this sort of abstraction and of reclusion in his
own affair, this sort of profane monasticism.
And as were the scholarship and art of the Renaissance, so was its philosophy. Philosophy
again! Would that there were some one word
for the wisdom acquired from letters as the
record of human experience — the kind of
learning that is not erudition or scholarship,
certainly not metaphysics, but " the knowledge
of the best that has been thought and said in the
world," the kind of thing to which Matthew
Arnold attaches the terms *culture* and *criticism*
almost indifferently! Such a word would be a
designation of Montaigne's humanism — with
reservations, for Montaigne himself is somehow guilty of that channelization of interests of
which I have been accusing his colleagues. He
too displays something of the same indifference
to other provinces than his own. He inclines to
make a rhetoric of life — that sort of rhetoric

which Plato classes with cookery, cosmetics,
and sophistry as one of the four impostors —
there is so much that he leaves out and slurs
over. Whatever he may say, he does virtually
shelve the Church. The ease with which he sets
it away in the cupboard and turns the key upon
it, for safe-keeping ostensibly, while he goes
about his business, argues no very profound or
vital religious or moral convictions. Consider
by contrast Pascal's desperate anxiety for the
very matter that Montaigne is quite content
to take for granted, provided nothing more need
be said about it. Evidently his heart is not in
it or he could not keep his tongue from it as he
does; it is hardly more than a skeleton in the
closet where he has ceremoniously deposited
it. His culture is as dilettante and amateur as
the corresponding virtuosity; it is more or less
at second hand and affected — a collection or
florilegium. To us — well, to some of us who
have been inoculated at some time or other
with the virus of Puritanism such a state of
affairs seems unconscionable, that a man
should undertake to maintain two or three es-
tablishments simultaneously. No doubt men
do so and are able to live at peace with their
neighbours and themselves by a species of hypocrisy or self-deception; there is something

after all in a decent mid-Victorian pretense. But that one should vaingloriously own to a wife in duress and several mistresses at large seems a little shocking even nowadays when it begins to look as though this were the very direction in which we are retroceding. The dismemberment of consciousness, the violent sequestration of art and poetry from ethics and conduct, the cult of aesthetics and the indulgence of vice, the cant of education and the encouragement of illiberality, the veneration of research and the contempt of tradition — these and a thousand other anomalies are evidence that we are none so consistent and conscientious ourselves after four or five centuries of Protestantism and have still a use for a little comfortable casuistry which will enable us to dream complacently in a very untidy bed. And this or some such is not improbably the reason that Montaigne continues to hold his own and is even capable of inspiring a new translation for a new time and a new people.

What remains to such a spirit, the Montaignesque genius of disenchantment and inconsequence, its sole spring and well of impulse as its source of pleasure, is curiosity. And curiosity, for all that may be said to its advantage, ingeniously as Matthew Arnold may discriminate against inquisitiveness, is essentially unmoral. " La curiosité est vicieuse par tout," says Montaigne himself. It is whimsical and capricious; what it may happen to attach itself to, is unprognosticable. It is insatiable, and unscrupulous in the gratification of its appetite. Its sole incentive is amusement. It has no principles but a kind of logic, what Jowett called neither an art nor a science but a dodge. Without an occupation it is as likely as not to find its entertainment in gossip; and without a subject it is more than likely to cocker its self-conceit with introspection. And confessedly this is Montaigne's chief charm for his admirers, the charm of chat, of personal confabulation — "*le pauvre Montaigne*," as Pascal calls him rather morosely, with his little vanities and whimsicalities, his ironies and insincerities, his toys and pastimes. "*Le pauvre homme!*" And yet that in his case so much of the enjoyment happens to be intellectual is so far forth to the credit of his admirers as well as his own. In the words of Callicles, "What! do you think that I or any other man soever does not believe that some pleasures are better than others?"

Pascal

PASCAL is the last of the great Christian pessimists; and now that the churches have become on the whole as officially optimistic and humanitarian, if not quite so frankly worldly, as industry itself, I have thought it worth while to consider in him what I believe to constitute, with dualism, the most characteristic manifestation of the genuine religious consciousness.

Blaise Pascal was born at Clermont-Ferrand, June 19, 1623. He was the third of four children, one of whom died in infancy. The other two survivors were Gilberte, who became Mme. Perier, and Jacqueline, who took the veil as Sister Sainte-Euphemie. In 1631 the father, who belonged to the " nobility of the robe," sold his charge and removed to Paris for the sake of educating his son. There he became a member of the scientific society of the capital and in particular of the reunions at Mersenne's which formed the germ of the Academy of Sciences. A man of great intelligence, skilled in mathematics and versed in physics, he had unusually definite ideas on the training of youth. His main concern seems to have been to arrange a natural gradation or evolution of studies parallel with his son's mental development. But the young Blaise's precocity frustrated to some extent his father's plans. The latter had reserved the study of mathematics until his son should be fifteen or sixteen years old. But one day he happened to surprise the boy, who was then only twelve, occupied in demonstrating for himself the thirty-second proposition of Euclid.

As a matter of fact his education ended by being mainly mathematical in accordance with his own and his father's bent. Naturally he knew Latin, to which he added a little Greek; he could probably read Italian; and he was acquainted with the science of the day. But his literary having was small and his reading narrow — a few books and those well thumbed; in theology and metaphysics he was a tyro, relying upon his Port-Royalist friends for what polemical ammunition he needed in this kind. His spirit was formed on geometry. At the age of sixteen or seventeen, the time set by his father for his initiation into the elements, he wrote an " Essay on Conic Sections," which ravished Leibniz. And a year or so later he invented a calculating machine. It is in connection with the construction of this machine that he seems to have felt his first reserves toward the geometrical syllogism as an instrument of living truth or persuasion and to have conceived his first respect for that free play of the intelligence which he was to celebrate under the name of *finesse*. The moment is in this respect one of the turning points of Pascal's career and is worthy of a study which I am not enough of a psychologist to give it. I can only observe that his standard of truth has begun to change and that in the correction or control of these two principles, methodism and dilettantism, one by the other is to be found the secret of his apologetic style and power. From 1646 to 1648 he was occupied principally with his experiments to show that the suspension of a column of mercury in a tube is due to the pressure of the atmosphere, so disposing finally of the old personification of nature and her abhorrence of a vacuum. This again was an important date in his moral experience for it was the occasion of his first brush with the Society of Jesus. In 1651 as a result of these studies and reflections he published his treatises " The Equilibrium of Liquids " and " The Weight of the Air."

But as I have said, Pascal had already conceived a suspicion of demonstration and the demonstrable. Science was not sufficient to fill his being. And by this time he had undergone what is known as his first conversion, though it was but partial and incomplete. The manner of it was providential. In January, 1646, his father, having fallen on the ice and dislocated his hip, had put himself into the hands of two gentlemen living near Rouen, who were remarkable for cures of the kind. As it happened they were Jansenists. And the books of devotion which they lent him, made a profound impression not only upon him but upon his children also. As a consequence they concluded, in the spirit of Port-Royal, to renounce their traffic with the world, and Jacqueline, who was still unmarried, would have entered her noviciate at once, if her father had not refused to part with her. As it was, she lived in the spirit of her vocation, though at home, till his death in 1651, when she was finally received by Port-Royal. With Blaise, however, this first religious crisis was of short duration. By 1649 he was leading a thoroughly worldly life, a friend of the Duc de Roannez, *grand seigneur,* the Chevalier de Méré, *honnête homme,* and Miton, the " libertine." To this period and these associations must be referred the development of his ideas of *finesse* or the free play of the intelligence in matters of human nature. At this time, too, he produced his curious "Discourse on the Passions of Love," an exercise, as it were, in psychological appreciation. And a little later he returned to mathematics with his treatise on "Numerical Powers," in which he is sometimes credited with having anticipated the differential and integral calculus. Indeed, so far was he gone in vanity by this time that he even thought of securing a charge and marrying.

Nor was his escape far short of miraculous. In 1653 he was struck by a great light, which revealed him to himself in all his emptiness and futility. And this was not all; not only was the vision repeated with greater intensity and conviction in 1654; but the effect was confirmed, so the legend has it, by an unmistakable dispensation. One day, as he was driving, *en grand train*, with four horses — or was it six? — the leaders were frightened and jumped from the bridge of Neuilly. Destruction had been certain, if their harness had not parted at the instant, leaving them free to plunge into the stream, while Pascal remained hanging on the brink. It was this incident, whether authentic or not, which is responsible for the story of the abyss which he is said to have seen yawning at his side for the rest of his life. However this may be, it is certain that in 1655 he applied for a cell and entered into retirement at Port-Royal in the Fields.

While yet a boy he had been affected in health by the severity of his studies. From the time he was sixteen, so it was said, he never passed a day without physical suffering. During his first conversion the lower part of his body was well nigh paralyzed and he was unable to walk without crutches. In the interval he had recovered to some extent, but by a singular coincidence he was ailing again when he made his retreat. From that date his decline was rapid. After a last spasm of intellectual activity, in which he found energy enough to conduct the Jansenist attack upon the Jesuits with his masterly " Lettres Provinciales " (1656–1657), he broke down completely. Nevertheless he occupied himself in his stronger moments until his death on April 19, 1662, with the affairs of Port-Royal and his project for an apology of Christianity, jotting down on slips of paper or dictating the notes which were afterward collected under the title of " Pensées " and which form, fragmentary though they are, the most imposing monument or cairn to his genius.

There is a disposition — natural enough, perhaps, under the circumstances — to rate the Pascal of the " Pensées " as merely an epigrammatist, remarkable for the audacity of his sallies, but without very much coherence or consequence. For one who thinks of him as a geometrician, a master of severe and symmetrical demonstration, there are ninety-nine who see in him only the brilliant and spasmodic aphorist. To consider his performance in any such piecemeal fashion, however, is to mistake it seriously. In spite of the name, which is a concession on the part of his early editors to a seventeenth-century taste, the " Pensées " are by no means elucubrations in the manner of La Rochefoucauld. They are memoranda toward a projected apology of Christianity — fragments, therefore, incomplete in themselves and unintelligible without some larger view of the whole in which they were intended to cohere. Strip Pascal of his dialectic, reduce him to the *rôle* of a rhetorician, consider him only as an expression, however able, of the vague instinctive aspirations and terrors of humanity; and you have missed the point and endangered the perception of his significance. At bottom he is neither natural philosopher nor poet, but controversialist and churchman; and his import, which resides in his moral and religious consistency, is traceable, not in the several items of his *Nachlass,* but in the general conception of the apology.

But there is another reason for the popular estimate beside the fragmentary condition of his masterpiece. A perverse generation, with small sense of religion, a moral consciousness thoroughly bewildered, and a distracting smattering of physical and social science, can hardly be expected to discover in Pascal's divine contempt for common sense and solemn plausibility aught else than its own questionable relish for paradox and equivocation. Montaigne is much more to our liking. He is neither doctrinaire nor " superstitious." You can go with him a mile without the risk of being obliged for the sake of consistency to go twain. You can pick him up and set him down when and where you will. In short, he is no more serious about things of the spirit than we are. And the only faculty whose exercise he requires is the sort of every-day canniness which distinguishes between the worse and the better end of a shrewd bargain.

For after all Pascal has lost his case. The moral and religious reform for which he stood has foundered. Jesuitism and Pelagianism have triumphed in spite of him. We are all quietists and casuists of sorts nowadays. We believe in the self-sufficiency of humanity and the accommodation of the church and the world. The Society of Jesus, which he threw into temporary confusion, was only a skirmish line; hardly was it dispersed when Christendom moved up in force and occupied the position from which it had been driven. Religion has become thoroughly secularized. Its professors have learned to apply the methods of Escobar to the reconciliation of philosophy, science, literature, business, and the thousand and one mundane interests which were once regarded as inimical or fatal to its existence. And at the same time the sects have returned by a parallel movement to the ancient humanitarian heresy condemned by the early councils.

But let Pascal himself define the situation. It is not the object of the Jesuits, he says in the fifth of the " Lettres Provinciales," to corrupt good manners. " That is not their design. Nor is it their sole aim to reform them; that would be poor policy. Their idea is this. So good is their opinion of themselves that they believe it beneficial and even essential for the welfare of religion that they should extend their credit into every corner and govern every one's

conscience. And since the severe instructions of
the Evangelists are suitable for the governance
of some kinds of persons, they make use of them
wherever applicable. But as these same instructions do not suit with the views of most people,
they set them aside in such cases in order to
satisfy all the world."

Such is the policy which had only to be
clearly stated to arouse the indignation of the
seventeenth century. And such is the policy
which meets with general approval nowadays
— the design, that is, to keep as many people
as possible within the pale of some church or
other, regardless of their individual beliefs and
convictions — to attract and retain as many
customers as possible. In order to accomplish
this feat, however, it was necessary in that day
to fulfill two conditions; it was necessary in
the first place to shuffle aside the awkward doctrine of efficient grace, which was a stumbling-
block to the imperiously willed and the worldly
minded, and in the second place to make religious discipline itself light and tolerable. The
first object was attained by the ingenious inventions of sufficient grace and proximate
power. The point of these logomachies of the
Molinists lay in the fact that they restored a
measure of natural virtue to humanity at the

same time that they saved the letter of the dogma. Whereas efficient grace involved man's total impotence and depravity, and attributed his conversion entirely to God's will and pleasure; both sufficient grace and proximate power declared his ability to act for himself and to promote or hinder the operation of the Holy Spirit without being in themselves completely adequate to his salvation. Hence Pascal's scoffs at a sufficient grace that is insufficient and a proximate power that is quite powerless.

Over this musty old theological quarrel, however, it is unnecessary to linger, especially as Pascal himself took no great part in it. It is thoroughly antiquated by this time. The churches, like the state, have become too democratic and humanitarian to tolerate the privilege of divine election or endure an aspersion of human virtue. It is interesting only to notice that in spite of Protestant abhorrence of Romanism religious opinion has marched up and seized the outposts which Catholicism was once disputing with Arnauld and the Jansenists.

Aside from the doctrinal, there was still a moral aspect to the matter. If the direction of the Jesuits was to be made acceptable to the greatest possible number, it was essential to ease its yoke. And to that task also the Order, with the help of their friends the Casuists, addressed themselves. It would take too long to enumerate all the happy expedients with which they were inspired; but as such expedients were intended to have the force of practical rules of conduct, it may be worth while for the sake of comparison to mention one or two of the most remarkable.

First and foremost, then, was the notable doctrine of probable opinions or " probabilism." In accordance with this conceit any opinion expressed by a doctor of theology was to be considered " probable," unless expressly disavowed by the Church, and might as such be followed with a clear conscience even when less probable in itself than another. In this fashion two diametrically contrary opinions might be equally good and authoritative, and the tender churchman might follow which suited his occasions the better. While further, a confessor was obliged by the rules of his order to absolve a penitent if there was a probable opinion in his favour although it might appear improbable to the priest himself. To take a single example, which Pascal has wrenched a little in his own sense. Filiatius, the casuist, debating the critical question whether " he who has spent himself in running after a woman is under an obligation to fast " as usual, answers, " In no wise." But if he has fatigued himself expressly to avoid fasting, shall he be held to it? " Even if he has done so on purpose," replies the learned father, " he shall not." Such constitutes a probable opinion and the sinner may conduct himself accordingly.

From this notion of probabilism it is but a step to the general notion of the indifferency of all opinions which prevails to-day — certainly among Protestants. Again the Jesuits have anticipated us. The popular conviction that it makes no difference what any one thinks about man or God or devil; that the more numerous the opinions and sects and the more diverse and individual, the richer the religious life; that ideas and beliefs and principles are of no consequence, that a Christian is a Christian whether or no — what is it but an extension of the casuistical theorem that one opinion is virtually as good as another?

But this is not all. When probabilism fails to make religion easy and comfortable, there is another lenitive — the directing of the intention. As guilt dwells exclusively in the motive, it is quite possible to commit a crime innocently by thinking of something else while you are perpetrating it; in other words you may direct your attention elsewhere to some object legitimate or praiseworthy in itself. So a man may kill a false witness, not in anger or for the sake of revenge, but in order to preserve his property from the effects of the other's perjury, since the protection of property is in itself a laudable end. Or a man may pay for a benefice with the idea, not of buying it — that is a mortal sin — but merely of inducing the holder to part with it. Or a son may wish his father dead, in the hope, not of getting rid of him, but of coming into his inheritance. — But this is all so commonplace in a day when fortunes are made by hook or crook solely for the sake of endowing libraries and universities and hospitals and churches that I am ashamed to expatiate upon the subject. Who of us has not heard of a peculator's being recommended to mercy because he stole, not for the sake of thievery, but of keeping his family in comfort, to say nothing of our tenderness for murderers? Indeed, as Sainte-Beuve pointed out long ago, some of the instances that Pascal singles out for reprehension have become such matters of course that his indignation is no longer intelligible; for example, the contention that " an act is not a sin when it is involuntary and devoid of intention formally evil." Such is the validity of the

"common notions" to whose infallibility
morals were once referred.

Nor is the practice of avoiding offense by a
liberal interpretation of awkward or objection-
able doctrine much less familiar. Pope Gregory
XIV had refused the right of sanctuary to
assassins; whereupon the casuists promptly
interpreted assassins to mean only " such as accept money for killing some one treasonably;
whence it follows that those who kill gratu-
itously and merely to oblige a friend are not
assassins." This is a little extreme, perhaps; but
it is on the same principle that we are encour-
aged to put our own construction upon ecclesi-
astical doctrine and keep our own counsel. A
few mental reservations, a slight equivocation
or two, a poetic imagination, and a liberal use
of metaphor and mythopœa; and the trick is
done. It is only a little while since a journal of
great gravity in religious matters took the Protestant Episcopal Church to task for suspending
one of its priests who was so unfortunate as to
be unable to accept the creed. The Church, declared this organ of enlightened religious opinion, should allow its members to attach
whatever meaning they please to such phrases
— indeed, it must do so sooner or later if it is
to continue in existence and do business as

usual, I suppose. What a training, as we say, for citizenship! For "if gold ruste, what shal iren do?"

Such, then, is the condition of affairs in Christendom at large to-day. Under the circumstances, when we have come to build upon the ruins of Pascal's outworks, it is no wonder that appreciation for the consistent and systematic religious thinker should have given place to admiration for the inconsequent aphorist whose incoherent utterances are more agreeable severally with the temper of the times or can be made to seem so. Nor is the work of restoration in itself without difficulty. To pretend to collect from the scattered memoranda of the "Pensées" the author's complete design would be bare-faced intellectual fatuity. Their very order is subject to doubt and dispute. And they are so sparse and random that any total reproduction of the original conception is quite conjectural and untrustworthy. And yet while its economy on the whole eludes our question, it is possible to detect the larger outlines of the system, to apply idea to idea, if not text to context, in such a manner as to clarify our own rather dubious latter-day notions of religion by the settled convictions of the last great apologist of Christianity.

Whatever is doubtful about the execution and details of his design, the leading motive, the pivot on which it turns, is clear. It centres inevitably, as every such attempt must centre, upon the fundamental duality of human nature, the glory and the abjection of man. Denuded of its mythological and theological trappings, in what else does the religious sentiment consist than in this ambiguity or duplicity of feeling, a profound conviction of human impotence and misery on the one hand and on the other an equally profound conviction of human grandeur and elevation? Retrench one of these factors and religion ceases to exist. Grant that man is all of a piece, all one thing or the other; and together with the split in his nature there disappears also the conflict of good and evil, the sense of duty and sin. His vices and virtues become merely civic and social. The whole history of the inner life, that record of intestinal dissension and strife, becomes unintelligible. Man is no longer a religious but an economic and scientific creature.

Naturally such a polarity of consciousness, founded though it may be in the dualism of our being and supported by the common-sense distinctions of mind and matter, spirit and flesh, soul and body, is intolerable to the vanity of reason. It is a mystery. But while religion, frankly accepting the evidence, undertakes to produce a kind of temporal order, if not unity, by repressing the lower instincts and desires and encouraging the higher, metaphysics and science, on the contrary, attempt to evade the dilemma altogether by ignoring one or the other of its terms; whereas art and literature, in turn, though starting from the same immediate postulates as does religion, proceed in a contrary direction in seeking to perpetuate the sensuous and the secular to the prejudice of the spiritual and the eternal. Hence the hostility of religion to science and art. They are both irreligious in one way or the other — Plato was right; and it is only an age of religious weakness or indifference that tolerates them, much less applauds their boasts that they, too, are religious in their own fashion.

Such, at all events, is the point that Voltaire, who seldom deceives himself as to the key of the enemy's position, selects, as skeptic and "libertine," in his attack upon Pascal. "With respect to Pascal," he writes, " the problem hinges upon this question — whether human reason suffices to demonstrate a double nature in man." Pascal's originality, however, consists, not in the mere affirmation of this re-

ligious commonplace, but rather in the vividness and immediacy with which he has succeeded in realizing the fatal dissension so
that he seems in the end only to be confirming
our own sinister suspicions. Protest as vociferously as we may — and we shall protest
vociferously or not at all — the very vigour of
our protestation is a kind of confession. Even
Voltaire's sonorous challenge — " I venture to
take the part of humanity against this misanthrope sublime; I dare assert that we are
neither so wicked nor so wretched as he declares " — even such high language fails wholly
to drown the disheartening echoes that Pascal
has raised in the recesses of our conscience.

Indeed, such and no other was his intention
— to appeal from the clamour of the mind and
the senses to the still small voice of the inward
witness; to array, if need be, our apprehensions
and nightmares against our waking reason. " A
writer often sets down matters which he can
prove only by obliging every one to turn his
reflections upon himself." And as a matter of
fact, never was the underlying pessimism of
religion, the sense of worldly bankruptcy to
which the prophet appeals, more firmly grasped
and more surely rendered. With a certain feeling for relief he has not spared a shadow that

might darken the background of mortality
against which he intends to contrast the bright-
ness of celestial grace. By character man is only
a dissembler, a liar, and a hypocrite — " How
hollow is man's heart and how full of ob-
scenity! " — while his condition is one of in-
constancy, ennui, and anxiety.

" The nature of egotism and of this human
ego," so says Pascal in one of his developments,
" is to love only self and to consider only self.
But how then? Man can not prevent this object
of his affection from being full of faults and failings: he wishes to be great and he knows himself little; he wishes to be happy and he feels
himself wretched, to be perfect and he is riddled
with imperfections, to be the mark of men's
love and regard and he sees that his shortcomings deserve only their aversion and contempt. This quandary in which he finds himself
inspires him with the most unjust and criminal
passion imaginable; he conceives a mortal
hatred of the truth which confounds him with
his own faults. He would like to annihilate it;
and unable to destroy it in its principle, he
destroys it, as far as he can, in his own consciousness and in that of others. In short, he
takes pains to disguise his vices to his neigh-

bours and himself; he can not bear that they should be seen of himself or his fellows. . . .

"So it follows that man is only seeming, falsehood, and hypocrisy. He does not want to be told the truth; he avoids telling it to others. And all these dispositions, so far removed from justice and reason, have their natural root in his heart."

Indeed, so great is the deception and the instinctive detestation of truth that "if all men knew what one says of another, there would not be four friends left in the world"; nor must it be supposed that even "when people have no interest in what they are saying" they are not lying still, "for there are those who lie simply for the sake of lying."

But bad as is our private character, our public morality is even worse. As a matter of fact there is no such thing as justice or equity; it is all usurpation and force of one sort or another. At best justice and morality are only custom and acquire all their authority from imagination.

"Nothing, reasonably considered, is just in itself; everything changes with time. Custom is the only equity for the sole reason that it is received; it is the mystic foundation on which the authority of justice rests. He who follows it to its principle destroys it. Nothing is so faulty as the laws which redress faults; who obeys them as though they were just, obeys an imaginary justice but not the essence of the law: the law is all gathered into itself, it is law and nothing more. Whoever were to examine its motive, would find it so slender and feeble that if he were not used to contemplating the prodigies of the human imagination, he would be amazed that a century had lent it so much pomp and reverence. The art of 'fronding,' of overturning states is to shake established customs in probing to their source. It is necessary, so the saying goes, to return to the fundamental and primitive laws of the state which have been abrogated by unjust custom. It is a sure way of ruining everything; nothing would weigh in such a balance. The people, however, gladly give ear to such talk. They shake off the yoke when they recognize it; and the great profit thereby to their ruin and that of curious scrutators of accepted customs. It is on this account that the wisest of legislators used to say that for the good of men it was necessary to fool them. It is necessary that they should not feel the reality of the usurpation, which was introduced aforetime without reason and has ended by becoming reasonable. It is necessary to have it considered authentic and eternal and to conceal its origin unless you wish it to come to a close forthwith."

And in completion of his political or civic theory, which is curiously suggestive of Montaigne and Plato at once, the following passages are not unworthy of comparison : —

"It is well to heed right; it is necessary to heed might. Right without might is powerless; might without right is tyrannical. Right without might is subject to contradiction, for the wicked are always with us ; might without right is denounced. It is essential, then, to unite right and might, and for that purpose to make right mighty and might right. — But right is open to dispute, might is easily recognizable and indisputable. So it is impossible to add might to right because might has disputed right and asserted that she herself is right. And hence, since it is impossible to make right mighty, we have made might right."

And in the following *pensée,* according to Brunschvicg's arrangement, whose edition of the "Pensées et Opuscules" is the best and most convenient for the general reader:

" Doubtless, equality of goods is just: but being unable to make force obey justice, we have made it just to obey force: not being able to enforce justice, we have justified force — in order that justice and force be of one side and there be peace, which is the sovereign good."

And finally:

" Why does the majority rule? Because they are more likely to be right? By no means — but because they are the stronger."

Such are the creature's character and civilization, and his natural condition and fate are hardly more reassuring.

" Imagine a number of men in irons, some of whom are massacred daily before the eyes of the others, so that the survivors see their own condition in that of their fellow victims, and looking at one another dolorously and without hope, await their turn. Such is the image of human life," for " the last act is bloody however fine the rest of the comedy. In the end cover your head with dust, and there you are forever." At best " we ought to look upon ourselves as prisoners in a dungeon, filled with images of their saviour and with the instructions necessary to their escape from bondage."

But it is in his theory of pleasure or diversion withal that his conception of the inanity within and the confusion without assumes its darkest and most woebegone expression. As an illustration of the kind of patching by which several fragments may be pieced together into a fairly consistent argument, the passage would be worth quoting. But in addition the idea is a persistent one; it is one to which Pascal returns again and again. And as such it serves to support an interesting conjecture with regard to his psychology — or more correctly, perhaps, his physiology.

" When I have set myself from time to time to consider the various agitations of men, and the pains and perils to which they expose themselves, at court or in war, whence spring so many quarrels, passions, and difficult or even evil enterprises, I have discovered that all the misfortunes of man result from a single cause — that he is unable to sit still in his room. A man who has enough to live on, if he were able to enjoy himself at home, would never leave for the sake of going to sea or following a campaign. No one would buy a grade in the army at so high a price if he did not find it unendurable to remain in town; and no one would seek for society and play if he were not unable to stay at home with pleasure.

" But after thinking more closely and finding the cause of all this unhappiness, I still wished to discover the reason of this cause. And I have found a sufficient one in the misery natural to our frail and mortal condition, which nothing can console when we think of it closely.

" Whatever position be considered, if all the goods which can possibly pertain to us be collected, royalty is the finest station in the world. And yet observe even a king accompanied by all the satisfactions which are proper to him, if he is without distraction and is allowed to ponder and reflect on what he is, his languid felicity will not sustain him; he will fall of necessity into the views that threaten him, of revolts that may arrive, and finally of disease and death which are inevitable: so that if he is deprived of what is called amusement, he is unhappy, and more unhappy, if anything, than the least of his subjects who can play and amuse himself.

" Hence it is that gaming and sexual intercourse, war and high office are so much sought after. It is not that they constitute happiness in themselves, or yet that any one imagines that genuine happiness consists in possession of the money that may be gained in play or of the hare that is coursed. It is not the easy and comfortable possession that leaves us free to think of our misery, which we desire — or the dangers of war or the cares of business; but it is the bustle and confusion, which prevents us from this thinking with its violent distraction.

"It is on this account that men so love a noise and a stir; that prison is so horrible a punishment, and that the pleasure of solitude is something incomprehensible."

"So unhappy indeed is man that he would distress himself, even without a cause, by force of his own disposition, and so frivolous that though full of a thousand adequate reasons for distress, he is diverted by the least little thing such as playing billiards and knocking a ball about."

"This man here, so afflicted by the death of his wife and his only son, who has this great quarrel on his hands, how comes it that at this moment he is not contrite and sad and that he looks so free of care and anxiety? It is not surprising: some one has served him a ball and he has to return it. . . . How can you expect him to think of his affairs, having this other business to manage? There's a concern to occupy a great soul and banish every other thought from his mind."

Grim as this is — pitiless as is this wholesale devastation of our flimsy toys and even flimsier make-believes, it does not pass, I have ventured to think, without wringing a kind of reluctant acquiescence from our gloomier and profounder moods. It is merely an expression of the pessimism proper to the religious instinct; and to say that Pascal possessed it in unusual fullness is only to say that he was religious in unusual measure. Indeed, for all his earlier worldliness, there is not a little in his later temper, the temper of the " Pensées," to recall that of the Puritans, though without their starved and impoverished imagination and defective culture. We are all likely enough to become Puritans and penitents in the dead watches of the night and early morning. But the Jansenists, with whom Pascal had identified his religious interests, were protestants and reformers as well by vocation. Their peculiarity was that they would have reformed the Roman Catholic Church from within; while they agreed with the Calvinists as to the Augustinian dogma of grace, they differed with them irreconcilably in their views of the Eucharist.

But at all events they protested vigorously against the growing relaxation of manners, particularly among the clergy and religious orders. And what is more significant from this point of view, they attempted to rehabilitate the religious idea in its purity; they insisted upon the absolute incompatibility between the religious and the worldly life, between piety and " honesty." Pascal's father had always been a respecter of religion even in pursuing his affairs; and he had inspired his son with the same sentiment, in which religion had, as it were, an honoured place apart. But even though Pascal himself had never withdrawn his hand from that of the church, his conversion dates only from his retreat, when says his nephew, Étienne Périer, " he showed so plainly that he wished to quit the world that the world finally quit him." It was in pursuance of this uncompromisingly religious purpose that the Jansenists, naturally enough, ran foul of the Jesuits, who were the great composers, the opportunists and expediency men of the day, and although their efforts were abortive on the whole, they did succeed in ruining for a time the credit of their adversaries as a society.

It is not astonishing, then, that these Port-Royalists, dissidents and schismatics as they were, including Pascal, should resemble in some respects their " heretic " contemporaries across the Channel or refuging in the Lowlands. A note preserved in manuscript speaks of Pascal in these suggestive terms : " M. Pascal was marvellously apt in concealing his virtue — so much so that some one or other remarked one day to M. Arnauld that M. Pascal always looked to be wroth and on the point of swearing." Ironical? Whether or not, the allusion to his propensity to righteous indignation arouses some reflection, particularly when Pascal is found confessing it. " I couldn't help it," he says on one occasion. " I'm so provoked with those who will have it that their reasonings are truth." The temper of reformers is not always the most equable or equitable; urbanity, affability, hesitation are not precisely their affair. And however conciliatory Pascal may wish to seem or may actually feel as an apologist, he can hardly escape the methods of his *métier*. He must appear harsh, rude, absolute. He must amaze and shock and confound the sinner. And this unavoidable procedure is alleviated by little of that Christian infancy, the simplicity and naïveté of the new birth, which is illustrated so admirably by Saint Francis of Assisi. On the contrary, he is sophisticated, intricate, *rusé*.

He represents an age in which skepticism was beginning to close with faith, and the struggle is bitter, relentless, and not invariably scrupulous. His ingenuities and subtleties, his whole arsenal of paradox and antithesis, his ambuscades and countermines come after a while to look suspiciously oblique and strategical.

Naturally the aspects of Christianity to recommend themselves to a character of Pascal's sort, were not always what we should now regard as the most amiable and attaching. In a genuinely religious consciousness there are, humanly considered, great gulfs and bottomless abysses at which we seldom glance in this profane humanitarian age. The very notion of a religious mystery is obnoxious to common sense and abhorrent to general sentiment like a qualm or a treachery of nature, which has appropriated all the divinity man has to spare. While to our worldly wisdom there is no cynicism so reprehensible as that which condemns the very terms and conditions of our present existence. Indeed, the compromise which Pascal was trying to arrest, the concordat between church and world, has gone so far by this time that it is necessary to do ourselves a kind of violence in order to reconcile his position with sanity. The world a prison, life slavery, hu-

manity but excrement — how foreign and out-
landish to the indulgent ecclesiasticism, the
comfortable complacency, the divinization of
impulse and instinct, the veneration of nature
and the natural, the apotheosis of humanity
which passes for religion to-day! Compare Pascal's haughty contempt, not only of the general
intelligence of the race, but also of human culture and the painfully wrung conquests of right
reason, a sentiment in which we are, perhaps,
too much inclined to agree with him as far as
tradition is concerned — but then what is our
tradition if not Christian? — so that after all
the consensus is, as might be expected, more
apparent than real.

" Original sin is folly before men, but then it
is posited as such. You ought not to reproach
me for the unreasonableness of this doctrine,
since I posit it as unreasonable. But this folly
is wiser than all the wisdom of men, *sapient-
ibus est hominibus*. For without it what can
man be said to be? All his state rests on this
imperceptible point. And how should he perceive it by his reason, since it is contrary to
reason, and since his reason, far from having
originated it by its own means, shies away from
it when presented."

Such is his high-handed manner with the intelligence. And it is this, perhaps, more than anything else, which is likely to shock the modern reader — the freedom, namely, with which he admits the irrational into his argument. It is not so much that he represents the ways of God as inscrutable and his faculties as incommensurable with ours — or in rational language, that he concedes so large a place to the incalculable in human affairs. But it is rather that he converts this very element of doubt and perplexity into an evidence of truth, much as a mathematician might work with irreducible or indeterminate factors.

" The prophecies cited in the Gospel — do you think them reported for the sake of making you believe? Never; but to prevent you from believing," for " it is impossible to understand the works of God save on the principle that he has made them to blind some and enlighten others." Hence no proof is thoroughly convincing unless it is ambiguous. " If God had allowed only one religion, it would have been too easily recognizable; but when you look more closely, you detect the truth in this confusion " so that " all seeming weaknesses are forces " and the truth of religion is discernible

" in the very obscurity of religions, in the little
light we have in us, and our indifference to
knowing it."

In short, it is the uncertainty of the premises
which constitutes the strength of the conclusion. Is it too absurd to be believed, it must be
true; otherwise, it would have no sense at all—
it is too ridiculous to be false. Mahomet is a
false prophet because he was successful; — and
intelligible, we may suppose, in himself. In
such wise Pascal has perfected, if not invented,
a new instrument of controversy — the argument from absurdity. For to see in all this ap-
paratus of apology nothing more than a questionable turn for paradox, is to see with only
half an eye. It is a logic, the logic of unreason,
which he gradually developed and which constitutes in one sense his greatest claim to
originality. Handled properly, it is irresistible.
And in fact, so sure of it does he feel himself
that he does not hesitate to stake his whole
case upon it. " All these sacrifices and ceremonies " of the Hebrews were " figures," he says,
meaning that they are to be interpreted meta-
phorically and spiritually of Christianity, or
else they were " follies." Either skepticism or
Christianity — such is the pass to which he is

eager to bring the whole matter. Christianity or nothing; there is no other alternative. And it is in view of just this dilemma that he undertakes his impeachment of human reason, happiness, and justice. For I can not agree with Sainte-Beuve that he was ever seriously unsettled by Montaigne. Agreeable as Montaigne is with our own disposition, there is something so obviously trifling about him that it is impossible to take him quite·seriously even nowadays. He is so evidently dealing with only one side of the problem, he omits so patently one set of data altogether. It is only that Pascal found in him the other term of the antinomy for which he was looking to complete his own scheme — the universal negation complementary to Epictetus' universal affirmation. That Pascal is right is undeniable — in pushing his argument to an extreme however dangerous — in view of the fact that nothing has been more fatal to Christianity than the attempts of its friends to rationalize it. It is Tennyson of all others whom Huxley welcomes as an ally. They are both engaged in the same work — the reduction of a religion to an aestheticism, a beautiful and hazy sentiment like a vaporous aureole surmounting life without intruding upon it, a mere poetry, an idle play of the imagination. But such is not the attitude of a vigorous apologist like Pascal. If Christianity is supernatural, it is only by repudiating common sense, he concludes, and denying its competence that his cause can be defended.

Nevertheless the great doubt, which is never admitted, against which every chink and cranny are stopped, is always imminent. If this world should turn out to be right after all; if the issue should justify, not Pascal, but Montaigne and Gallio? For once find a contestant bold enough to admit the alternative and take the part of folly, how shall he be refuted? Nor is Pascal himself quite at ease in his convictions. His spirit is disquieted within him. He has not wrestled with the skeptics without having his withers wrung. He is subject to dark misgivings and gloomy apprehensions. He has glimpses of appalling vistas far below our horizon. And he is filled with fear and trembling. "The eternal silence of these infinite spaces terrifies me."

There is, to be sure, another side to the dualism which composes the religious nature of man; but it has not been etched so deeply. Nor need it be, since it is more likely to be taken for granted by the complacency of human nature, while doctrinally it is less important since man is subdued to his surroundings and habitation. But none the less there is a divine principle somewhere about him; otherwise, would he still be hopeless of salvation. In spite of his degradation and depravity there is in him something superior to his own character and his circumstances; for all his humiliation he has a soul above it and himself. Bubble though he is on the stream of eternity, he is not wholly immersed in it. Himself a vain shadow in a world of illusions, he has the power to detect and expose the cheat. Complex and inconsistent creature though he is, still there is a single element at his centre whereby he holds of the divine. Were it not for this, were it not for his living like a transitory guest in a dilapidated tenement, a ghost haunting the ruins of a tragedy, his nature and destiny would be incomplete.

"Man is only a reed, the frailest reed in nature — but a reed that thinks. It needs not the whole universe in arms to crush him — a vapour, a drop of water is enough. And yet were the whole universe to destroy him, still would he be nobler than his assassin; for he knows he dies, but of the advantage the world has of him it knows nothing."

"Man's grandeur consists in his knowing

himself wretched. A tree does not know that it is wretched."

" All his miseries prove his grandeur; they are the miseries of a great noble, of a king dethroned."

And in words that sound strangely like Hamlet's, " What a chimera, then, is man! What an anomaly, what a monster, what a chaos, what a subject of contradictions, what a prodigy! Judge of all things, imbecile worm of the dust, depositary of truth, sewer of doubt and error, glory and refuse of the universe! "

These, then, are the two faces of the equivoque, which forms the basis of the apology, the one inseparable from the other and complementary to it. In this restless oscillation of spirit from one pole to the other, from passionate aspiration to melancholy dejection at the dark disastrous vision of mortality which looks from the modern point of view morose beyond the usual measure of Christian cynicism, it is difficult not to see something morbid, unhealthy, pathological.

That a philosopher or a moralist should have found the contemplation of self, even when we grant the worst to introspection, quite so intolerable as Pascal makes it out, seems at first

thought incredible. Montaigne did not find it
so. Nor is it credible that the admirers of those
who like Socrates and Plato have proposed self-
knowledge as the end of wisdom, which is happiness, should do so either, though it may be
that the Socratic dialectic was a kind of outlet,
after all, for that insufferable inward ennui, of
that need of outward business and distraction
that Pascal describes — seeking relief in the
jostle of dialogue. At the same time it is necessary to remember that however weak and ailing
he may have become in his later years — so
much so that he was often unable to rise from his
bed or trace his notes for himself ; yet his physical infirmity is not necessarily a cause but only
a condition of his exasperation with humanity.
It is in the disgrace of the body that the faint,
half-stifled cries of conscience, of which he
made himself the transmitter, have the best
chance of being heard. It is always by a con-
currence of circumstances, confirming and ex-
aggerating the natural bent, that the genius is
made.

And then, too, while his health was preying
upon his spirits, his austerity was likewise rav-
aging his flesh. It is a mistake to suppose that
the character of the ascetic is insensibility. To
some natures, on the contrary, asceticism is a

form of voluptuousness — certainly, a mode of
dissipation. If pushed, the mortification of the
body causes a kind of exquisite irritation, not
unlike that which results from indulgence in
pleasure and equally liable to revulsion. Like
every excess it has its own intoxication and
retribution. On occasion, therefore, what we
intemperately call virtue may be quite as morbid as vice. Nature is no purist; she fails to
discriminate. The effect of either extremity is a
condition of abnormal nervous excitability and
exacerbation, a derangement of vital function
— in fact, just such alternated fits of exaltation
and collapse, of enthusiasm and prostration as
those between which Pascal's mood veers. It is
on these two poles that his world turns; and
their foundations are deeper than any reasoning, they are rooted in the subsoil of his being.
It was probably on this account, therefore, as
much as anything that he accepted Christianity in the more rational sense — not as a faith, I
mean, but as a theory; because the dogma of
the fall, of original sin, and of redemption
seems to fit into this crease in his consciousness,
scored and deepened as it was by his conditions
and circumstances. "The true religion," he
says in a short fragment, "must teach grandeur and misery; it must incline to the es-

teem and the contempt of self, to love and to hate."

At bottom, then, he acquiesced in Christianity, as Cardinal Newman did, because it presented a system of ideas agreeable with the constitution of his consciousness. As usual his passions furnished the pattern of his faith. And it did not occur to him that these conceptions might be mere projections of an inward dissension into the outward world where they do not belong. He did not see that they represented an attempt to reduce consciousness to its lower level, to confine humanity to the sensuous and the sensible; that they were, as a matter of fact, art or science, and hence essentially unreligious if not irreligious; that in any case they were the result of a mental confusion. For while religion in its essense, the religion of Socrates and Plato, rests upon a profound conviction of the ambiguity of human nature as such, while it is fundamentally moral and rational, the temptation has always been to prolong this split in consciousness beyond the human heart into the world at large — to enthrone a god upon the clouds and inter a devil in the bowels of earth, and to drape the universe in an intricate and voluminous cosmology and mythology. And I confess that when Pascal has once entered this limbo I begin to grope after him with fascination and dismay.

As a matter of fact, when divested of that operation of grace which looks like a mere gratuitous embellishment, the whole fabric of his argument resolves into two distinct strands — the natural and the supernatural. By the former, however, is not to be understood the usual argument from " nature " in the physical sense, the evidence for a so-called " natural religion " or deism. The irrelevance of such an argument Pascal perceives with his habitual penetration. " If a man were to conceive that the properties of numbers were immaterial and eternal verities and themselves dependent upon a primary verity in which they subsisted and which he dubbed with the name of god, I should not think such an one very far advanced toward salvation; " for " the God of Christians is not simply an author of geometrical truths and the order of the elements — that is the portion of pagans and Epicureans " so that deism is "pretty nearly as remote from Christianity as is atheism" — indeed, atheism and deism are " two matters which Christianity abhors equally."

It is not to nature, then, in this sense, to external nature, that Christianity must look for confirmation, but rather to human nature, to the consciousness and experience of the individual and the race. Such an argument is unanswerable pragmatically. As far as a religion justifies itself to my needs and aspirations, confirms my resignation, elevates my thoughts, consoles my griefs — in so far it will seem true and no attack of any kind can disturb or unsettle it. This wall of the apology, therefore, is the strongest and firmest. It establishes Pascal as a profound moralist and analyst of the human heart.

Small wonder that in the thoughts of this enthusiastic and agitated spirit, tottering on the brink of infinity, there should be much to disconcert those who live composedly retired from the verge. The wonder is that with so much to trouble and distract him he should have been so sharp-sighted in matters wherein more phlegmatic thinkers are quick to befuddle themselves. It is not astonishing that La Rochefoucauld and La Bruyère should show themselves shrewd, even sagacious moralists, living in the world and conversing with it as they did. But whence did Pascal, the geometrician and recluse, get his knowledge of the intricacies of human nature? His sages were Montaigne and Epictetus. The Chevalier de Méré and the Duc de Roannez were his men of the world. His

capital idea is St. Augustine's; his method is
Montaigne's. But what he makes of all this
is his own. Let the ordinary man have such like
advantages and he would make nothing of
them. And the difference is qualitative. The
genius is usually a simple, narrow-minded creature. He has studied but few books, known but
few people who have had any influence on him,
and he has but few ideas. Decompose him and
you can hold his dust in your hand. His great-
ness is an affair of intensity. The magic which
he spins he draws like the spider from his own
bowels. His experience is with himself. And so
in Pascal's case what constitutes the originality
of his book is the agony of his religious feeling,
together with that singular clairvoyance which
such ecstacy produces. It is comparatively easy
for the mere aphorist, who is always given the
benefit of the doubt, to hit or appear to hit the
mark every now and then. But to exhibit and
illustrate consistently, without obscurity or
confusion, the few plain and elementary truths
that form the basis of morality and the moral
nature is quite another matter. Even Montaigne, to whom Pascal is indebted for not a
little, and who generally faces the facts that
confront him, is not wholly guiltless of shuffling with the idea of evil — not as Marcus

Aurelius does, to be sure, and Emerson and the other moral amphibians; but still he does apply to it a sort of dissolving casuistry, after all, in hopes of refining away its realization if not its reality. For the Pagan there is, of course, only one honest way with death — to acknowledge it the worst as the last of evils,

" So weit die Sonne leuchtet, ist die Hoffnung
     auch,
Nur von dem Tod gewinnt sich nichts! Bedenk'
     es wohl! "

and as such to be endured with what fortitude he can muster. But the attitude of the Christian is a peculiar and in a manner an anomalous one. Spiritually he is bound to consider it the greatest of blessings, as an escape from prison, clouded only by a doubt of his own election, just as he is obliged to regard it after the flesh as the deepest of afflictions — an emotional paradox which is by no means inconsistent with Pascal's habitual mode of thought. But aside from this particular of death, which illustrates the fashion with which the severest philosophy coquets with its ideas, Pascal's whole system depends upon an unblinded recognition of the reality of evil, not as an accident but as an element of the constitution of things, ingrained in the fibre of life, and an unflinching acceptance of its consequences. Evil is the one certain and incontrovertible fact of existence upon which his structure is erected. "It requires no great elevation of soul to understand that there is no real and solid satisfaction here, that all our pleasures are only vanity, that our ills are infinite, and that finally death, which threatens us every minute, will infallibly in a few years reduce us to the horrible alternative of being eternally annihilated or wretched."

The actual potency of evil, the frailty of our nature, and the hollowness and insecurity of life — these form the one axis of his morality. The other is the accountability of the individual. Brushing aside the fatalism that might seem a corollary of his doctrine of grace, he riddles the flimsy pretexts by which humanity attempts to evade the consequences of its own folly and mischief. With the various fallacies that would divorce thought from action or plead the natural law in bar of the moral he has scant patience. Man acts as he thinks at his own risk and peril — to his own damnation — even though his damnation be brought about by God's contrivance, who has made his testament "to blind some and enlighten others"; for after all " each but finds what is at the bottom of his own heart," and though we are saved by grace we are damned by our own concupiscence.

And indeed, it is only by clinging desperately to some such conviction that we can preserve the integrity of the moral order at all. Once admit sophistication into our conceptions of personal responsibility, once blot or blur the great elemental fact of evil, once lay the blame of our evil-doing upon nature or society, once teach the indifferency of ideas — and our moral downfall is assured. No amount of ingenuity or power or eloquence can compensate for disorderly thinking. Depravity resides in the head as well as in the heart; and the only security for the soundness of our affections is the clarity of our thoughts. Pascal is right in implying that good behaviour depends on a correct estimate of the desirability of one course of action or another — that is, upon clear ideas. At all events such must be the case in a fallen state of nature. And it is in accordance with this principle that the moral appeal of the apology is calculated. We like a thing because we are used to it; we become attached to it, we say. It is as easy to form a good habit as a bad. And if we would fall in love with virtue, we must begin by frequenting her. To act as though a creed were true is the best means of coming to believe in it. Man is more reverent on his knees than on his feet. Faith, therefore, is finally an affair of the affections; it is the sanction which the heart accords to an inclination approved and initiated by the intellect and the will. " It is the heart that sees God, not the reason." All the reason sees is the desirability of God and religion. The point is to get it to see this desirability in the first place.

To obtain this result Pascal proposes the argument of the wager, which has shocked so many serious and conscientious souls by its sporting associations and which may be cited as an example of the audacity of his dealings with a wicked and perverse generation. To take the very lowest ground, every time we act we are virtually staking our salvation on the existence or non-existence of God, the truth or falsehood of Christianity, since we should not act alike in both cases. This risk we can not avoid; we must bet either on God or against him, since not to bet at all is in reality to bet against. Hence it behooves us to consider the odds. If we bet on God and Christianity — that is, if we act on the assumption of their truth — we stand to win a stake of infinite value, eternal blessedness, no matter how small the chance of their being true. If we bet against — that is, if we act as though they were false — though we should win all the world, our advantage would still be finite, as would also be the chances against God and Christianity, since there is at least a chance in their favour. In other words, the sportsman will venture at all events for God as representing a disproportionately larger gain; he will take the longer odds, if so be, for the larger stake, though Pascal curiously enough does not appear to see that the size of the stake does not affect the probabilities one way or the other, or else does not credit his gambler with the ability to see it.

Such an argument, while it smacks curiously of bookmakers and actuaries, was no doubt effective at the time for the kind of man for whom it was intended — the man of the world who is already used to this sort of speculation, and in the midst of affairs where certainty is out of the question is inclined to take long odds of opportunity. But what is more important at present, it includes a kind of error to which all this sort of appeal is liable and from which Pascal himself did not escape. It is calculated for an age in which the presumption is all in its favour and it takes advantage of that assumption. If faith is, as Pascal contends, an habitual

manner of thinking and acting in which reason
has acquiesced and to which the heart has
finally become attached; then, whether this
condition be raised to a state of grace or not,
it is evident that no ingenuity can escape from
the errors incidental to the representations by
which the intellect was first reduced. In other
words, behind Pascal's belief lurks the assumption that Christianity is true already, just as
behind our criticism to-day lurks the suspicion
that it is doubtful. As a result, not only Pascal's mathematical calculations but his noblest
pleas have lost their cogency; if they appeal to
us at all, it is no longer religiously but ethically,
expediently. For in one form or another this
same fallacy is always cropping up. Faith is
finally an affair of inspiration. Those who believe in Christianity, therefore, are inspired
whether they have read the Scriptures or not
or whether they have any knowledge of the
prophecies and miracles or not. Whereto, naturally enough, " it will be answered that the
heretics and the infidels will say the same: but
I reply we have proofs that God actually inclines the hearts of those he loves to believe in
Christianity and that the infidels have no proof
of what they say." And in his Preface to the
" Abrégé de la Vie de Jesus-Christ " occurs a

like passage equally characteristic of this spirit. Of his attempt to " harmonize " the gospels he remarks, " If the reader finds anything good in it, let him thank God for it, who is the sole author of all good; and for what is faulty let him forgive my infirmity." In other words, what happens to be correct is good ground for faith and what happens to be wrong is merely evidence of human fallibility and as such is equally good ground for faith. It would not take a mathematician to count the chances with the dice so loaded.

The fact is that in spite of his remarkable skill in manœuvring Pascal has turned his own position. If faith is a matter of inspiration, then is argument irrelevant first or last. It is possible only to note a difference of opinion and go our ways in peace. And such is exactly the strength of his position, had he been contented to remain entrenched in it. He would then have avoided the necessity for a supernatural proof altogether. But that he could not bear to do. Montaigne, in establishing a skepticism of the intellect, in confuting human intelligence, and in leaving religion entirely to faith, had proved all that is capable of demonstration. He had left Christianity to subsist, if it could, as a spiritual affair, acceptable in as far as man finds it accordant with the inner life, a matter of personal experience and individual concern. Pascal, however, was not content merely with reviving and sustaining what Montaigne had left on one side to take its chances; he must reinstate it as a fact of the physical as well as of the historical order, a cosmology, not merely an ideal and an inspiration. Hence the need of an entirely different order of argument, the argument from prophecy and miracle, which leads him for the sake of doubtful and impermanent advantages to strip his strongholds and high places.

With this change of front, it need hardly be said, he loses at once the mastery of the situation, which depends not upon the course of cosmical evolution but upon the constitution of the human spirit — at least for those generations who are not in tacit agreement with the traditional assumptions at the bottom of his argument. For it is evident that the whole theological proof stands in the same case, say, as the question of Moses' good faith, which is one of the piers of his supernaturalism. Once discredit Moses' existence, and the fall of man will have to stand on its own feet. No doubt it would form, if proved, an interesting confirmation of man's depravity. But how if it is disproved? It is simply a question of fact; and to-day the depravity of human nature is more patent than the fact. In short, Pascal has deceived himself and begun to trespass upon the preserves of science and literature; and history and criticism have in so far disabled him. To integrate religion with the physical order is beyond his powers; he can only postulate it after the fashion of his time. Ancient speculation is still valid in as far as it consists of an ethical interpretation of life, a free play of the intelligence about our spiritual experience. But whenever that philosophy has tried to smuggle in an explanation of physical fact, it is antiquated, as antiquated as last year's science. Knowledge is not wisdom. From the latter point of view Socrates — or was it Plato himself? — was perfectly right in renouncing the study of physics and preferring man to nature. And so it is that Pascal's value will be felt increasingly to consist, like that of Socrates and Plato, in his profound and powerful divination of the heart of man in its confrontation with the mystery and illusion of life.

" I know not who has placed me in the world, nor what the world is, nor what I am myself. I am terribly ignorant of everything. I know not what are my body, my senses, my soul, or even this portion of me which thinks what I am saying, which reflects upon all things and upon itself, and yet knows itself no more than all the rest.

" I see these frightful spaces of the universe wherein I am enclosed, and I find myself fixed in a corner of this vast space without knowing why I am put here in this place rather than another, or why this trice of time I have to live has been allotted me at this instant rather than another of all the eternity which precedes and follows me. I see only infinities on all sides, which enclose me like an atom and like a shadow which endures but a moment and is without return. All that I know is that I have soon to die; but what I know the least is this very death from which I can not escape."

This is his ground; it is on this footing that he is unassailable.

SIR THOMAS BROWNE

WHILE thinking of Montaigne and Pascal, I have often wondered how Sir Thomas Browne would have fared — the French make so much of their writers — if he had been born across the Channel. We identify him as the author of " Religio Medici "; but the " Religio," mainstay of his reputation as it is, has never been taken very seriously save by a few virtuosi of style like Robert Louis Stevenson — if that sort of taking may be called serious at all. Is it too much to assume that if it had been French, it would have received in measure the same sort of intelligent attention as has been the portion of the " Essais " and the " Pensées," from which it is separated by no great interval of time and with which it has certain obvious analogies? If these three writings are dated approximately — the three recensions of the " Essais " at 1580–1588–1595 (Florio's translation into English being published in 1603), the " Religio Medici " at 1635, and the " Pensées " at 1660 — their propinquity is evident. The wonder is that Sir Thomas should seem so much older than the Sieur de Montaigne, who antedates him in reality by more than half a century. Is it the former's religiosity that makes him appear relatively so antiquated? But then Pascal does not suffer from the same embarrassment? Is it his Anglicanism? Or is it the naïveté of the scientific mind, for I suppose that a disposition naturally scientific will be conceded the physicians even of those days?

And yet in spite of his apparent anachronism, which may be the effect of our own perspective as is the case with those other men of science, Newton and his prophecies, say, in comparison with Sir Oliver Lodge and his apparitions — however this may be, the three of them at all events — Montaigne, Browne, and Pascal — taken together serve to route the last great retrograde movement from skepticism to enthusiasm, with the " Religio Medici " as a kind of intermediate stage or stepping-stone. Not that there have been no later instances of the temporary discomfiture and retreat of reason — mystic, obscurantist, superstitious, idealistic, even rationalistic — but none with so much genius behind it, none so opportunely timed and so ably generaled. Whatever else, Pascal was a great tactician. And although no

one will maintain that Sir Thomas Browne oc-
cupies any very exalted position in the history
of thought or even that its main stream ever
passed through him — while in short he is only
a term of comparison by which we may measure others, as he derives his interest from
them; yet it is an interest and as far as it goes
a genuine one.

No matter for the instant in what direction
they severally head when once on the way, the
problems which the three of them set out to
solve are very similar. They aspire to nothing
less than a complete philosophy of life. They
undertake to say what they themselves and by
implication what every one else should think
of this, the most vital of all subjects. They are
concerned with conduct as influenced by conviction, for they were quite untouched by the
modern belief in the indifference or irrelevance
of ideas. They were all of them occupied with
thoughts of God and the soul, of dissolution
and immortality; for religion was still the province of divinity and a matter of life and death,
and not as yet "social service" or "big
business."[1]

[1] Lest I should be accused of irreverence or flippancy, I
hasten to quote two excerpts — the first from a daily paper in the
month of August, 1926; the second from E. Belfort Bax's con-

With regard to the supreme importance of these topics they all agree; it is their starting point. But Montaigne, I believe, abides by his original doubt and indecision, in the skepticism which is but the beginning of wisdom. Religion is to all intents and purposes extruded. Nominally, to be sure, it is reserved to faith and revelation, whose deponents, the heart and the Church, are in consequence withdrawn from the uncertainties of discourse and the agitations of dispute. In point of fact it is dismissed with all sorts of circumstance and ceremony; but none the less is it out of court and debarred from any participation whether as counsel or witness in the trial of experience over which Montaigne is presiding. With Pascal, on the contrary, it is the reason which is finally debarred deliberately and definitely with that

---

tribution to the Second Series of " Contemporary British Philosophy."

" Criticizing modern aspects of the church, he said, ' from Roman Catholic to Unitarian, religion is big business.' "

Never mind the antecedent of " he "; it is not imporant.

" Thus the social side of Christianity generally, especially in the alleged teachings of Jesus, is deliberately exaggerated, and introspective precepts, presented with a social colouring which there is every reason to believe did not originally belong to them."

I am not sure about the grammar, but there is no doubt about the sense.

relentlessness which used to characterize the Christian apologist. While Sir Thomas Browne's singularity consists, English-like, in the will to compromise, to bring about a practical reconciliation or working agreement between the two parties. Or should I say between the three; for as a Protestant or Anglican he is in a position to recognize a third voice in the controversy — revelation, authority, and common sense? " In brief," he declares, " where the scripture is silent, the church is my text; where that speaks 'tis but my comment; where there is a joint silence of both, I borrow not the rules of my religion from Rome or Geneva but the dictates of my own reason." And he observes aphoristically but not quite ingenuously, " Every man's reason is his own best Œdipus."

Such is his deposition. Its intent is in one sense just the opposite of Montaigne's. As Montaigne professes his faith and confesses his reason, so Browne professes his reason and proceeds to confess his faith. His philosophy and Montaigne's are accordingly counterparts; what the one suppresses the other proclaims. But at the same time he differs from Pascal in making no overt attempt to browbeat the intelligence, though as a matter of fact, since he actually ignores it, the effect is not very differ-

ent albeit the impression rather resembles Montaigne's discretion in diplomatically excluding
inconvenient visitors. As a result the " Religio " does virtually recognize a divorce between religion and reason, and on the principle
that the absent are in the wrong raises a presumption in favour of the respondent. In the
one instance as in the other the case is allowed
to go by default. All matters, so Sir Thomas
Browne, that do not come within the competence of faith, whether in revelation or authority, revert to the reason; but since his faith is
equal to pretty nearly anything, except his own
medicine, there is little enough left anyhow and
that little is in the main morally indifferent —
mostly, as far as he is concerned, physiological.
It is the familiar scientific subterfuge, which
enables the rationalist to save his face, while
professing his orthodoxy, by the simple expedient of keeping two sets of books, one or the
other of which may be a dummy. But whoever
originated the notion — and its respectability
ought to be evidence to its age — Sir Thomas
Browne, in adapting it to his own occasions,
has the distinction — I will not say of founding
but of anticipating what may be called the
modern method of rationalistic apologetics.
Granted that Browne is intent upon divinity;

he is not totally blind to the possibility of making providence responsible for necessity and then turning necessity to account in illustration of providence — divinity working through law, god immanent in nature, and therefore negligible or not as may better serve the turn.

Such is Sir Thomas Browne's contribution to that rather anomalous creation of human ingenuity — theocratic science. In one way and another it has helped many a scientist out of a tight place, having proved particularly useful to the evolutionists, and the biologists generally. Possibly Montaigne had a hand in leading up to it; but in fairness the trick should go to Browne, himself a man of science and a confessor. To be sure his sophistic appears to us a little inchoate and somewhat confused with foreign elements of one sort and another. It is impossible, for example, to read him for any length of time without observing that he is quite as anxious for theology or dogma as for the secularized or laicized religion that we nowadays call Christianity. In characteristic fashion he confounds Aristotle and the Apostles. And since he takes his metaphysics on trust, the substantial interest of his tract, aside from its methodology, consists in its measurement of his suprasensible acceptances and the aspect that the miraculous assumed to him. On this point it must be acknowledged that he appears not a little superstitious, though comparison with the modern " spiritualistic " scientist is still in his favour. There is something about all this modern spiritualism or " spiritism " for which, loth as I am to use the word, I know no other epithet than obscene. But while Browne expiates freely in the marvellous, he succeeds on the whole, if not wholly, in escaping this miasma. He has a kind of wonder-mongering streak in him and when a mystery is wanting delights in inventing one. He believes in ghosts, witches, and evil spirits, in necromancy and the philosopher's stone. The exception, of course, is when the prodigy begins to trench upon his own profession; then he finds it quite impossible to credit the curative properties of relics, though he makes no bones about believing " that spirits use with man the act of carnality, and that in both sexes." The infantile credulity of these men of science and what a feeble prophylactic, for all their boasting, is their special knowledge — a veritable empiricism!

Clearly Sir Thomas Browne of Norwich is not as who should say an *esprit fort et endurci*. Possibly an intuitive recognition of the fact is responsible for his easy abdication of the intellect. He knows nothing apparently of the inner conflict that ravaged Pascal. " As for those wingy mysteries in divinity and airy subtleties in religion, which have unhinged the brains of better heads, they never stretched the pia mater of mine." Nor is he quite the liberal humanist either in the manner of Montaigne. Occasionally he seems to recall him in a personal remark: " I do not feel in myself those common antipathies that I can discern in others; those national repugnances do not touch me, nor do I behold with prejudice the French, Italian, Spaniard, or Dutch." But the resemblance is superficial. In fine, what he *thinks* is not of great importance for all his "vast learning." He was satisfied to confine himself within the bounds of the scholastic tradition. His mind was doctrinal rather than philosophic; in religion he found a pleasant field for the exercise of his ingenuity. How far it appealed to him as a favourable theatre for literary gymnastics, is an open question; but this or something like it has come to be his main attraction — he maintains for our delectation a museum of quaint archaic phrases and complex and intricate rhythms. In this particular it is suggestive that the first few pages of the " Religio " are more vivacious and diverting than the following as though he had amused himself hugely with his own ingenuities to begin with. And yet he scores less often than Pascal; his hits are less palpable and less profound. Even such remarks as, "I am not so much afraid of death as ashamed thereof," are comparatively rare. As a rule he is given rather to paradoxes and conceits: "Nay, further, we are what we all abhor, *anthropophagi,* and cannibals, devourers not only of men, but of ourselves; and that not in an allegory but a positive truth, for all this mass of flesh which we behold, came in at our mouths; this frame we look upon, hath been upon our trenchers; in brief, we have devoured ourselves."

On the whole, then, if we wish to make the best of him, it is by his imagination that we must take him. It is a sort of imagination characteristically English and as characteristically un-French, consisting not in the organization and clarification of thought but in the fermentation of language. De Quincey has it too, and to a certain unmistakable extent all the other great English essayists have it — with one or two exceptions like Addison and Lamb. On this account they are likely to be better poets than critics, though they often enough write bad poetry — or prose, just as you look at it. Their strength, like Browne's, is in the image, not the idea — in the perception of cunning figurative resemblances and verbal antiphonies rather than in the apprehension of logical relationships. It was in the clash and *mêlée* of words that he found his inspiration,

> " When elephant 'gainst elephant did rear
> His trunk and castles jostled in the air."

And there is still a pompous romance in his recondite Latinisms and his ponderous sesquipedalians and his labyrinthine circumlocutions, from which his sentences seem to clear themselves by a kind of grammatical legerdemain that baffles and outwits the intelligence of the reader. In speaking, for example, of the " reformed, new-cast religion," of which, he protests, he dislikes nothing but the name, he animadverts as follows upon the intransigent: " Yet have I not so shaken hands with these desperate resolutions who had rather venture at large their decayed bottom, than bring her in to be new trimmed in the dock — who had rather promiscuously retain all, than abridge any, and obstinately be what they are, than what they have been — as to stand in diameter and sword's point with them." As a *genre tranché,* no doubt, it leaves something to be desired; but to the English ear its merits are indisputable. It has volume, rhythm, resonance, intricacy, suggestion — everything save simplicity, measure, and clearness. In short it is in the great romantic English tradition from whose oceanic currents even Dryden never quite freed himself.

WHATEVER else may be said of the nineteenth century, it was at all events an unusually interesting, if not a thrilling age. " The century in which I have lived," says Renan, " will probably not have been the greatest, but it will doubtless be considered the most amusing of centuries." And in the life of the writer of these words, as it is to be drawn from his " Lettres Intimes " and his " Souvenirs," there are difficulties and problems of the most engrossing sort such as are unsuggested by the life of a man like Dr. Johnson. The internecine feuds of the spirit, the rapid alternations of revolution and reaction in every province of thought, the vortex of tendencies, flux and reflux, ebb and flow, systole and diastole, with the consequent unsettlement and fluctuation of opinion — these vicissitudes give the characteristic life and temper of the time, a life and temper like Renan's through whose brain was slowly distilled its main stream of speculation, an appeal which is as irresistible as it is curious. Here, for instance, at the very

moment when Renan was passing from one
pole of thought to the other, Newman was making the same transit in the opposite direction.

From a comparison of these two spirits,
thrown together in this manner in a fatal and
unconscious antithesis, it seems as though
there ought to be much to be learned. In their
ages there was about twenty years' difference,
so that the leaven which was at work in Newman, was already, as compared with Renan's,
a thing of the past. They were both fond of
mathematics — a significant trait, for it indi-
cates in both a taste for the *a priori*, a fondness
for abstract speculation, for air-tight ideal con-
structions impervious to external influence. Of
the force of such material or phenomenal evidence it is quite clear that Newman remained
unimpressed. To his mind an idea needs no
demonstration or experimental verification; it
carries its own proof. His test of truth appears
to have been logical validity; if a proposition
was self-consistent, it was true and therefore
real. Indeed, of objective reality or actuality it
is doubtful whether he had any distinct conception at all. Not only does he assume that a proposition which is intelligible is universally valid;
but he constantly speaks of his " distrust of
the reality of material phenomena." The visible

universe is to him a symbol — or rather, a gigantic veil bulging with conjectural shapes of truth but in itself unmeaning and in so far contemptible. Belief is not an elaboration of experience, but an apprehension of the soul. He "receives" a doctrine, not because it tallies with fact, but because it happens to agree with his temperament — because it strikes him, one is tempted to say, as an ingenious or otherwise attractive fabrication of the human spirit. Such is the character of Newman's mind, metaphysical and mediæval.

Although Renan has nowhere recorded his youthful attitude so completely, it is fair to assume of him, who began where Newman ended, that his early state of mind was very similar — particularly since this ideality, this speculative turn, to which he always pretended in general terms, explains his later conduct as well as Newman's. With both of them it was all or nothing. From the character of their minds they had little or no sympathy with the spirit of compromise, the political spirit, the spirit of business and what we call practical affairs. But on the one hand Newman was still haunted by the ghost of the past — that old romantic ghost of theology and scholasticism, which had been proving the existence of things

from their definitions and whose apparition
had driven a few superstitious Germans quite
out of their senses. In some such mind he was
able to disregard the world of fact altogether
and to remain perfectly satisfied with his her-
metically sealed systems of thought. On the
other hand, no sooner had Renan — animated
by the new wine of science and diligently check-
ing idea against fact — discovered or had
forced upon his notice the fallibility of his
speculative projections, than he threw the
whole fabric over in distaste, and lapsed, im-
patient of all brain-spun tissue whatsoever,
into universal skepticism.

Or rather, to speak popularly, it was not so
much skepticism into which he lapsed as a conviction that truth is too elusive for our theories
and formulæ, that it always lies, so to speak,
betwixt and between, so that however diligently
you may try to scoop it up with your little intellectual ladles, it will always escape you, or
else, conforming to the shape of your vessels,
will lose all resemblance to its source and original. And even if it were possible to catch the
general tone of truth, its shades would still defy
your pigments. The best to be done, perhaps,
were to take it at its poles and then multiply
your intermediate points of view. In this way

you will spin as close a mesh about it as may be. But as its facets are infinite, scrutinize it as you will, you will never exhaust its myriad refractions.

After some such fashion, then, Renan and Newman with something of the same cast of thought issue at opposite extremes; the one conceiving the search for truth to consist in a perpetual agitation or oscillation of spirit, the other in a fixed and inflexible posture and gaze. Nor is it, indeed, unreasonable to see in the rigidity of Newman's attitude an evidence that he too had caught a glimpse of that fluctuating and unstable sea whereon Renan was to embark, and terrified by the prospect, had preferred no matter what principle of authority so that it were strong and arbitrary enough to save him from the fate of the castaway and derelict.

To judge only from the surface of Renan's letters to his sister, Henriette, his first doubts would seem to have arisen over his vocation rather than his faith. But it becomes apparent on a little reflection that the expression is only a euphemism, that his belief has collapsed or is on the point of collapsing, and that he introduces his vocation for the sake of leading up to the serious problem, which he wishes to avoid for the moment. His desire, he says, is to live a quiet studious life in independence and self-accountability; and he questions whether such a life is what the priesthood has to offer him. This is the subject he pretends to discuss with his sister. They profess themselves offended by the self-seeking, the pettiness, the hypocrisy, the servility that they observe in many of his calling. They fear lest he too should lose his integrity and independence intellectual and moral. They dread lest he become a mere organ, a member of a body in which his individuality shall be obliterated. It is only when the correspondence is pretty well advanced, on April 15, 1845, that he speaks quite openly of his religious scruples, and exclaims frankly, " I haven't faith enough!" Nor do I see any reason for aspersing his motives or for regarding his hesitations in the light of a duplicity, as has frequently been done.

" As soon as my reason awoke it demanded its legitimate rights, such as every age and school have accorded; it was then that I undertook the rational verification of Christianity. God, who sees the bottom of my soul, knows whether I have done so with diligence and sincerity. In fact, how would it be possible to judge

lightly and frivolously [en se jouant] of dog-
mas before which nineteen centuries have pros-
trated themselves? Certainly, if I had to defend
myself for any partiality, it would be one
favourable, not averse to them. Did not every
consideration incline me to be a Christian?
Both my happiness and long habit and the
charm of a belief in which I was brought up
and with which my notions of life were saturated? "

Unquestionably he left the Roman Catholic
Church, decidedly to his own hindrance, for
the reasons he assigns; and for the same motives he declined to identify himself with any
other communion. " It was neither scholasticism nor philosophy that destroyed my faith,
but historical criticism." " This theory of inspiration, implying as it does a supernatural fact,
can not be maintained in the face of the definite
ideas of modern good sense." And " in a church
founded on divine authority one is as heretical
for denying a single point as for denying the
whole affair." Such is the order of ideas by
which he was influenced. Those who question
his intellectual honesty in this matter are only
incapable of understanding the force of objective evidence upon a mind of this sort in a time

like his. But happily it is no longer necessary to discuss at length the logic or psychology of doubt.

As for his delay in coming to a decision or at least to a clear statement of his position, an evasion of a kind it is, to be sure, but an excusable one in a case so serious, as long as human nature continues to take its difficulties at an angle and to allow them to slide past if they will rather than to meet them head on. And indeed, as a matter of fact, his consciousness was not so much equivocal as indeterminate; and for that his sister was partly to blame. And there, by the way, is a woman who deserves a study to herself as fully in her own way as Pascal's sister. She had no desire to see her brother a priest, had Henriette — quite the contrary. But she scruples to accelerate his steps on the road he is travelling. And if anything, her reserves appear to have retarded his progress. In fact, the whole psychological situation at the moment is a very peculiar one. But at all events it is unjust to accuse him of shuffling; it is rather the solemnity with which he takes his own case that is remarkable — not so much, perhaps, in a youth of twenty-one, for all young men are serious when alone; but in the arch-skeptic of the century to be.

For this one trait, apparently so inconsistent with his general character, Renan not only possessed at the time but retained in undiminished fullness throughout his life. He never doubted the importance of his own concerns. It is almost portentous, the gravity with which this young fellow takes himself and his future. Did it never occur to him, I wonder, in the uncertainty and bewilderment of youth that it might make very little difference after all what became of him as of any one of us? It would be interesting to know whether his late disciple, Anatole France, had made an advance upon his master at an equal age, and suspecting the futility of all prevision, had resigned himself to leave his future to circumstances. But with Renan apparently skepticism never led to such consistent personal indifferentism. And it is hopeless to expect to penetrate to the core of his case without explaining the inconsequence. With Montaigne the matter is perfectly clear. He was a writer, and in spite of his protestations he had the vanity of the artist. And I confess, it seems to me as though Renan were in the same boat. Certainly, he is unintelligible unless it is remembered that his consciousness, like his talent, was to some considerable extent a literary one, his own modest asseverations to

the contrary notwithstanding. Thoroughly " literary," for instance, is his " Vie de Jesus." He
was much concerned for the effect of the word,
the phrase, the whole form of thought. And his
impression does depend greatly upon his manner. It is an affair of shading. His work is a
work of temperament. And how greatly the
tinge of temperament is affected by a slight in-
fusion of skepticism, no one who has read him
carefully can fail to perceive. Is it too much to
suppose, then, that artist-like he was shrewd
enough to recognize and cultivate, either deliberately or instinctively, the quality which
gives his style its distinctive flavour? At all
events the development of this bent of his would
seem to countenance such a supposition — that
he was not less affected by the æstheticism than
by the historicism (if I may coin the word) of
his age. It would explain a great many things,
in particular that suspicion which I believe I
am not alone in feeling for the man while ad-
miring the author.

The suspicion that I speak of is not the sort
which one feels for antipathetic ideas, nor is
it exactly the suspicion of insincerity. It is
rather the natural distrust of an acquired accomplishment so assiduously cultivated as to
seem an affectation. One feels in something

the same way nowadays in this democratic country of ours towards a person who pretends to good manners. And what, indeed, is Renan's quality after all but manner, though it may be a manner which has become second nature? He has against him, whether justly or unjustly, the instinctive human dislike of artificiality. It is not the man whom we surprise in Renan but the author. In all this sort of thing, however, it is quite possible that some discount should be allowed the Frenchman. His characteristic must not be labelled deception or hypocrisy. To find a young man of twenty-one protesting " the sincerity of his heart," " the purity of his intentions," and the like, seems to the Anglo-Saxon an untoward circumstance — and in his case it might well be so. In the Celt, however, it may be only a touching evidence of sensibility.

In accordance with this view of his character it is still his manner in particular upon which the critics insist on pouring their praise. And rightly so, no doubt. But to my mind the tone of his " Souvenirs " and other confidential writings is not altogether agreeable. It is marked to my ear by a sort of *mollesse,* a moral flaccidity which wants in firmness and fibre what it gains in grace and flexibility.

" I understood but vaguely; and yet I had divined already that beauty is a gift so superior that talent, genius, and even virtue are nothing to it, so that a perfectly beautiful woman has a right to despise everything else, since she assembles, not in a work external to herself, but in her own person as in a myrrhine vase, all that genius sketches roughly and laboriously in feeble outline by means of painful reflection."

That is soft; it is flabby by the sentiment. And there is something in all Renan's style not unlike it. Nor is it unaccompanied on occasion by a trace — shall I say? — of vulgarity. He would be too clever, too enlightened, too knowing; and he succeeds as likely as not in being only fatuous.

" In fact I love only such characters as are absolutely ideal — martyrs, heroes, utopists, lovers of the impossible. With them alone I occupy myself; they are, if I may say so, my specialty. But I see what these great enthusiasts do not — I see, I say, that these great paroxysms are no longer of use and that for a great while now the heroic follies deified by the past succeed no longer."

There is about his mind, it is evident from the quotation, a curious mingling of astuteness and simplicity, of the secular and the spiritual peculiar to priests and clerics, and a disposition to make one retrieve the *niaiseries* of the other. He is so afraid of becoming another's dupe that he frequently becomes his own. He is at once too shrewd and too *naïf*. And the effect produced is, indeed, not very unlike duplicity.

To these traits the laxity of his tone is partly due. In part it is due also to that sort of desultoriness or volatility of spirit which he believed essential to the discovery of truth. But this volatility, which may in matters of the imagination become admirable under the form of wit, is likely in serious affairs to result in such a *rapprochement* or association of two or more topics incongruous to reason as to produce a dislocation of sense resembling inconsequence, or even worse, levity.

" M. Gottofrey, a young priest of twenty-six or twenty-eight, was, I believe, only half-French. He had the ravishing rosy face of an English miss, fine large eyes, from which emanated a melancholy candour. He was the most extraordinary example imaginable of a suicide by mystical orthodoxy. M. Gottofrey might surely have been, if he wished, an accomplished worldling. I have never known a man who could have been so loved by the women. He carried with him an infinite treasure of love. He felt the superior gift which had been bestowed upon him, since he taxed his ingenuity with a sort of rage to annihilate himself."

To be sure, Renan would be the first to disclaim any such æsthetic character as that with which I have been investing him. " I have always been the least literary of men," he protests, " I have never cultivated my vein." But to assume his veracity, it may be permissible for his readers to question whether there were not certain blind sides of his character where he failed to know himself — whether he had not, like Zola, his hallucination, too. The humility which he professes proves on examination to be of a unique sort. " I alone of all my age have understood Jesus and Francis of Assisi." Very complacent, too, almost Pharisaical, is he with regard to his own life and character.

" And so on the whole I have broken my clerical promises in next to nothing. I have abandoned spirituality for ideality. I have kept my engagements better than many priests who are very regular in appearance. In insisting on preserving in the world the virtues of disinterestedness, civility, and modesty, which are not applicable there, I have given the measure of my ingenuousness."

Whether just or not, it is again instinctive with most of us to feel a little reserve toward one who professes at the end of life, no matter how successful that life may appear to have been, that he has nothing to regret, save his virtues, perhaps, nothing to blot or cancel, nothing to improve or even change. "Taking everything into account, if I had my life to begin over with the right of erasure, I wouldn't change it." It smacks too much of an inhuman infallibility to engage our sympathies — or else it is unseemly quizzing. But his habitual self-complacency is not quite so immovable as it seems. Let age once shake his assurance and he falls into an unedifying strain of peevishness quite as disagreeable in its way as his early cock-sureness — for cock-sure of himself he is by disposition, so much so that virtue seems to him involved with his own being and to partake of its infirmity and dissolution.

" Conscientious as I am, I wished to be *en règle* with myself, and I continued to live in Paris just as I had done at the seminary. Later I saw the vanity of this virtue as of all the others; in particular I recognized that nature cares nothing at all for man's chastity."

A melancholy observation which might well arouse an honest man's pity, were there not a kind of perversity about it in the mouth of one who immediately confesses himself, in the gaiety of his heart and with an air of naïve self-congratulation, an agreeable and complaisant liar.

" I confess that in the early part of my life I used to lie often enough, not from interest, but from good nature, from disdain, from the false idea which always leads me to present things to every one in the manner in which he is able to comprehend them. My sister represented to me very strongly the impropriety of acting in this fashion and I gave it up. Since 1851 I don't believe I've told a single lie, except naturally merry lies [mensonges joyeux]."

In a word, if I may venture to voice my own suspicion — a suspicion which is only confirmed by a recollection of the contrast with Newman from which I started, I should say, in the tentative and guarded way in which alone such statements may be made, that what was antipathetic to Renan in Catholicism, after all, was not so much its dogma as its discipline.

A SOPHIST is one who denies in any way the duality of human nature and undertakes to reduce it to a single principle. As a rule he is nowadays a disciple of reason, a rationalist. He desires that everything should be made intelligible; everything must be explained and accounted for. This is his sole test of truth. What does not conform to this criterion, he denies and refuses to believe in. If it is undeniable, he tries to convert it into something else. Hence his indulgence for the instinctive; that is intelligible — at least it is part of the history of the race; and for a modern history is the only explanation. Ask him for a reason; and as Stevenson says, he tells you a story. So it is that the sophist is always trying to make it appear that human nature is merely an outgrowth and extension of physical nature. He defines humanity by the genus and omits the differentiæ. Man is but an animal, a natural object. Intuition is an illusion. Morality disappears or loses its sanction.

They are both inexplicable, unnatural, unscientific — impossible.

In this respect how like to some of Plato's sophists does Huxley often sound! In particular his little air of modesty and self-depreciation, his pretension to seriousness and fairness, as though no one had ever loved truth or sought it before. "It is only comparatively lately, within the last few centuries that the conception of a universal order and of a definite course of things . . . has emerged." Can this be ignorance or is it bad faith? For see how slyly, under cover of his protestations, he insinuates his poisonous little half-truth. "The possibility of all education (of which military drill is only one particular form) is based upon the existence of this power which the nervous system possesses, of organizing conscious actions into more or less unconscious, or reflex, operations." What is there about an utterance like this, a characteristic scientific utterance — yes, and a characteristically pedagogic one too — which makes it on the whole so false? In one sense it is correct enough, no doubt; but the impression that it produces is utterly misleading. The educated man is not the man of the greatest number of " unconscious or reflex operations "; quite the contrary, it would seem, is the manner in which he manifests himself in intelligent and deliberate action. Is it indeed the object of education to extend the province of the unconscious? If so, the cultivated man would be an automaton in the secondary and lower meaning of the word.

As contrasted with science, intuition is a direct and immediate apprehension of reality, that is, without the intervention of any formal method or system — either because the subject is incapable of methodization or because methodization is inadequate to express it. It is reality and nothing else with which intuition puts us *en rapport*. And it is the peculiar service of intuition to do so immediately. As a matter of fact, it is the worst of all systems that they fail at some time or other to report reality correctly. The case is notorious in literary criticism; the easiest way to miss the mark in criticism is to practise a method. That is scholarship. Even the man of science finds himself no better off in general for all his mastery of system; he is quite as helpless to deal with the significance of facts as an illiterate and makes mistakes equally absurd. In short, what he is handling is always a method, seldom a reality. His method is a banister which helps him down the one flight of stairs and leaves him to himself at the bottom. He may call this kind of thing thinking, just as hugging the coast may be called navigation, and he may beg the question by calling the free play of the intelligence guess-work; but at all events it is just this process-mongering which accounts for the fact that so many men of science to-day, the second genera-tion after Huxley, are such wretched writers — they are powerless outside of their techni-calities.

It is not, however, the mere notation or regis-tration of fact that intuition furnishes; it is rather its significance or import. It has to do with what reality means rather than with what it is — what it means at this moment, under these circumstances, from this particular point of view. And finally, it is just the interposition of method between such a conclusion and the reality itself which constitutes science. Science consists in the attempt to get a certain kind of conclusion from certain sorts of reality by the application to the latter of a certain invariable method. The application to a certain sort of fact of a rigid inflexible method is bound to produce a certain kind of conclusion. All others are obviously " unscientific " by definition. That is all the value and sense the word *un-scientific* has in such a connection. The conclusion is already prejudiced by the method; any other sort of conclusion is condemned beforehand. One kind of interpretation is fatally insured; and when nothing else comes through your sieve, you are told triumphantly that there is nothing else to come. Why? Because anything else is " unscientific "; namely, unscreenable. " The domain of science," Clifford assures us, " is all possible human knowledge which can rightly be used to guide human conduct." And yet perhaps if we screen long enough, something else will come through which even the scientists can not deny. But behold! it has taken the form of screenings like the rest of the scientific product; and they promptly take advantage of it to strengthen their own case, since they are unable to see anything which has not come through in just this way. So Clifford again: " To say: ' Up to this point science can explain; here the soul steps in,' is not to say what is untrue, but to talk nonsense." And in this manner they have had pretty much their own way with us for the last half-century or more without much difficulty.

Now this process of sifting with the notion of getting nothing but screenings forever, was not so bad, perhaps, when confined to nature or the physical world. But the moment that it was applied to human nature or the moral world, it began to be productive of the direst error. Morality, literature, art, religion — every moral and mental activity of man — have by this time been pretty well reduced to screenings, which are pointed to as evidence that there is nothing else anywhere, nor any other legitimate activity or faculty than that which makes screenings out of everything indifferently — namely, that " scientific thought," in the words of Clifford, " which is one thing with the progress of men from a worse to a better state." So it is to his formidable perch on this heap of screenings that man is indebted exclusively for his eminence. To quote the language of Le Dantec's " De l'Homme à la Science," " Physics, chemistry, practical sciences have, by their applications, made of man the uncontested king of the animals."

In a word, the fundamental assumption of science which gives it its peculiarly sophistical character is to-day as it was a generation ago the assumption that knowledge, knowing, is limited to scientific method, to scientific subjects exclusively. Yesterday Huxley animadverted upon " short-sighted scientific people who forget that science takes for its province only that which is capable of clear intellectual comprehension; and that outside of that province, they must be content with imagination, with hope, and ignorance " — a remark which, however relatively modest in its delimitation of science, is anything but reassuring in its promiscuous lumping together of imagination, hope, and ignorance. To-day Professor J. A. Thompson classifies human nature under three predominate moods: the practical mood, which accounts for the man of action; the emotional mood, which accounts for the artists — and I suppose for the authors too; and the scientific mood, which accounts for all knowing. Such is the assumption or presumption which has crept into all modern definitions of the subject. Science is the one means of securing truth, the one means of bringing the mind into contact with reality. " The classification of facts," says Karl Pearson, "the recognition of their sequence and relative significance, is the function of science, and the habit of forming a judgment upon the facts unbiassed by personal feeling is characteristic of what may be called the scientific frame of mind." The relative significance of facts! How does science recognize it, I wonder. And the formation of an unbiassed judgment! It sounds like sheer impudence.

Now, when to this conception is added the

further notion of philosophy as a criticism and systematization of scientific categories on the one hand and a synthesis of sciences on the other, the circumference of error is complete. There is nothing now admitted or admissible into the scheme except scientific knowledge — that is, screenings. To everything else is denied the credentials and title of seriousness. " Wir fordern für unser Universum," exclaims Strauss, " dieselbe Pietät wie der Fromme alter Stils für seinen Gott." (" We demand the same reverence for our universe as the old-fashionedly pious for their God.") All immediate moral perception, the free play of the intelligence is barred as an activity unworthy of any particular consideration in the plan of " holy Nature." To take but one example, what are our sociologists or political scientists so-called worth as compared with Burke? And yet Burke was eminently unscientific. Even in Bergson's opposition to science there is one scientific element that he fails to get rid of, and that the most vicious of all — namely, becoming. It is just the characteristic of science that it looks upon reality as something in process and never finished, a *werdendes,* a γιγνόμενον, a flux — call it *élan vital* or rheum. That is the mischief of it as a philosophy. And as long as Berg-

son enforces the same teaching, anti-intellectualist or not, he is in the same case — equally
mischievous and for the same reason.

The very fact that life is an illusion, that
about us there is as much chaos as cosmos, that
the universal process as such *is* a becoming, this
fact makes it the more necessary for man to
have a principle of fixity in himself — in
Goethe's words an inner hold. For this reason
every philosophy that seeks to reduce the
human spirit itself to fluidity, to make of consciousness merely a flux of sensation, to dissolve the fundamental conceptions and distinctions, is a mischievous and dangerous doctrine.
So Plato saw, and the spectacle drove him in
self-defense to his theory of ideas. For what
does Plato's theory amount to in the end but
that our real life is in thought, that the world
of appearances, of science, is but an illusion,
and that the only sense it has is given it by the
idea?

Certain it is at all events that there has been
developed in man a moral consciousness, which
is different from " nature " and superior to it.
Imperfect as humanity is, it is at least higher
than the physical order or disorder; it has some
elementary feeling for a difference between
right and wrong. To be sure, its discrimination

is by no means infallible. So frequent and so gross are its blunders that it might seem to have a natural disposition or inclination to error — as likely enough it has. But on the whole and in the long run it appears to have made a set of more or less reliable distinctions, which become in a manner the inheritance of the race, so that gradually good is disentangled from evil and truth from falsehood. In other words, there would seem to be a kind of reason or logos somehow engaged in the world — a moral and intelligible structure, if you like, expressed more or less clearly or darkly in the permanent acquirements or acquisitions of human culture. And yet in what jeopardy does any such attainment stand! How precarious these just discriminations! Consider only the manner in which human culture was overwhelmed in the Dark Ages and rescued by what appears a mere accident; how it was menaced by the Reformation; how it has been shaken by the French Revolution. And how of the World War as we like to call it? What distinctions made once may not have been confused since, while we immersed in our age remain in ignorance of our loss or even flatter ourselves upon our " progress "? For the idea of development, of opening discovery science has substituted that of evolution. We know or think we know that development and degeneration are complementary terms; the idea of evolution includes that of decadence. When will this development of our moral and reasonable tendencies cease and their decay begin? Perhaps it has done so already. Caught in the stream ourselves, how shall we tell whither we are moving? In any case how little reliance can be placed in such an evolution, the very goal of which is blind! How wretched a substitute for providence! And yet what else have all these modern scientific self-complacent humanitarianisms to offer us?

PATER

WE are putting the past so rapidly behind us nowadays that the authors of another generation have already begun to run together like an avenue of trees in perspective until we are hardly able to distinguish their relative size and distance. Posterity is a very uncertain court of appeal. The oak that once commanded admiration for its luxuriance has been displaced in our regard by some puny sapling in the foreground, and dwindled by time and space, is huddled with the elms and beeches of the past into an indistinguishable thicket whose members have all come to seem bewilderingly uniform and archaic.

On this account it may not be amiss to notice that Walter Horatio Pater, whose life in itself is immemorable, was born in 1839 and died in 1894. He had his schooling at Canterbury, whence he proceeded to Oxford. There he spent virtually the remainder of his days, as a fellow, up a flight of stairs in Brasenose, musing and bemused, with occasional breathing spells in

London and on the Continent. Such is his biography. His life was pretty much that of a recluse, a life of academic isolation and retirement. With the exception of a few tiffs with his colleagues, Jowett among others, due to incompatibilities of character and opinion, a kind of accident to which the scholar is particularly liable, it is remarkable only for its uneventfulness.

To the ardent young American of this generation, whose activities are inspired by the "ideals" of our great democratic universities, it is not even a matter of curiosity, I suppose, how the world looks to such a fainéant, whose being seems so little of set purpose, so merely casual and fugitive. A jumble of tones, colours, and forms, a checker of lights and shadows, a loose mesh of fleeting sensations and impressions like the surface of a painter's palette, a plaintive little air broken by distance and intervening noises, a smoke dispersing languidly in the breeze — such is the general sense of his consciousness conveyed by his biographer in the "English Men of Letters." And it is not belied by the evidence of his own writings.

Although he had been publishing in detachments, a contribution here and there for several years, the first volume of his own dates from

1873, the unlucky " Studies in the History of the Renaissance," the gentle hedonism of whose introduction and conclusion provoked a disproportionate squall of reprobation. He is not voluminous; his production seldom exceeded an essay a year. " Imaginary Portraits," " Appreciations," " Plato and Platonism," and " Miscellaneous Studies " just about exhaust the list of his titles — with the exception of " Marius the Epicurean," which appeared in 1885 and is undoubtedly his master-piece.

Not only is " Marius " a work of *longue haleine,* a unitary composition and not an aggregation of pieces; but it has also a peculiar significance for periods of transition and dissolution. Formally it is a kind of historical romance or biography. The hero, Marius, is a Roman patrician, born out of due time, during the collapse of the old Pagan world, amid the wreckage of its ancient creeds and customs. A man of elegant rather than vigorous aspiration, touched with a kind of Pateresque æstheticism, he halts between the severity of stoicism and the simplicity of Christianity, by whose seemliness he is attracted as by a sort of " comely decadence " though he is too much of a philanderer to commit himself to any one faith or philosophy and is content to die in much the same mind as he lived, an Epicurean and dilettante. Under the guise of this fable it is tempting to discover the traits of that moral and æsthetic enfeeblement which characterized the last decades of the nineteenth century and to which Max Nordau devoted a once popular study. Such at least was its interest for me when I first read it thirty-five years or more ago, and such is its interest for me still. Whatever the fiction, the spirit is modern and factitious and literary.

But however that may be, " Marius " remains a thing apart in Pater's repertory — unless we make another exception of " Gaston de Latour," which began as a romance of mediævalism but was never finished. On the whole, Pater was an essayist, to some extent a critic of art and literature, though most of his commentary of these subjects would fall under the head of appreciation, a term to which he has given the approval of a title-page. Of all his papers I prefer for what they are " The Child in the House " and " Emerald Uthwart," probably on account of their autobiographical aura. In so far I can enjoy his sensationalism — as a part of his own experience and suitable to the display of his peculiar gifts. Such exhibitions have an air of sincerity which is not infrequently wanting to what are avowedly the more disinterested and impersonal themes of a stylist. For it is to this ground that Pater owes his standing in English letters — his style or technique.

It is difficult to revive the freshness of a first impression. But to one who has never read Pater or his like before, the distinguishing characteristic of his writing is bound, I believe, to seem very like perversity. At least such is the effect it has upon the " plain man," of whose " naïve realism " the philosophers are making so much fun nowadays, albeit we were all plain men once and are so still with respect to a very wide range of subjects. From such a *tabula rasa* or clean slate whose " naïveté " makes him at least a better means of record than those of us whose surfaces are thoroughly scarified by all sorts of dubious experiences, I am trying to restore my sense of Pater's peculiarity, of that machined expression, so furiously at odds with the careless routine and businesslike convention of ordinary prose as to constitute in itself an unpardonable offense or irresistible fascination according to the disposition of the reader. As for the pure pleasure of it, it is to the title of an acquired and artificial taste, with whatever distinction such an accomplishment is thought to confer, that its appreciation pretends. So far from attempting to promote a free exchange between literature and life or to meet the plain man half way Pater, so he avers, wrote English like a dead, or at least like a learned language. And while there is in the present state of speech a good deal to be said for the practice, the result in his case is anything but conciliatory.

In a word, his rhetoric is pretty much a *tour de force*. His phrases are composed without regard for the natural trot of the human voice or the pulse of the human brain; they concur neither with respiration nor cerebration. Every period is a feat, a triumphant bout with grammar, which seems as though it could never be repeated. Nor is his discourse rectilinear; each member is a whirl or vortex, which, so far from opening out and flowing on into the following, tends to screw up into itself more and more tightly as it realizes its own perfection.

As a result his sentences, being deliberately manufactured, fail to represent not only the stream of consciousness but its individual moments as well. In its proper function a sentence is nothing more than the stereotype of a single state of consciousness, brought, for an instant, by the regular procession of thought, into the

immediate field of vision, to be at once succeeded by another. As such the sentence itself
ought to appear no more complicated than the
" specious present " happens to look at that one
instant. In other words, the faculty of making
sentences resides in the power of serial concentration and registration, a sort of literary
cinematography. But when the current of discourse is arrested on a period and the attention
is allowed to diffuse, then the sentence loses
definition and consistency with the moment
that constitutes it. All kinds of secondary considerations rush upon the mind and dispute for
the focus of attention. And if an attempt is then
made to introduce all this indirect visioning
into the construction, the result is a kind of
syntactical congestion or tumefaction.

" Since all progress of mind consists for the
most part in differentiation, in the resolution of
an obscure and complex subject into its com-
ponent aspects, it is surely the stupidest of
losses to confuse things which right reason has
put asunder, to lose the sense of achieved distinctions, the distinction between poetry and
prose, for instance, or, to speak more exactly,
between the laws and characteristic excellences
of verse and prose composition."

This is not such a monstrously long sentence, nor is it so very complex; but it illustrates the superfetation characteristic of the Pateresque sentence. The meaning is plain enough; it is a great pity to confound poetry and prose. But it suffers from over-exposure. The simple sense is so alembicated in the process of expression, it has undergone diffraction to such an extent that the sentence has finally ceased to be representative of anything in the nature of a *coup d'œil;* it is composition for its own sake.

For a rank outsider to define the attitude of a stylist to his art may seem not a little presumptuous. But from the instances that I have adduced it is clear that Pater at all events had come to look upon style as possessing a merit or virtue of its own, independent not only of life as such but of mind also — as it were a kind of conjury or magic. It is no mere medium of communication that he is straining to cultivate and perfect. Rather, the style is the idea, the idea is the style, just as the point of a trick is the trick itself. We of the commonalty of letters are prone to regard our phraseology as a vehicle or an accident of the thought. The stylist views his as substance, the thought is the accident; what thinks is the style. Style is the soul or entelechy of literature.

Of this curious æsthetico-literary mysticism
there lurks in my mind one ignoble suspicion
of which I can not rid myself. Can I be sure, I
find myself asking, that Pater ever intended
or foresaw all these exquisite effects and impressions, all this sensational and emotional
goose-flesh which his sentences actually produce? The process is so obviously experimental
and laborious, the product so intricate and consummate; it seems as though the deliverances
of soul should be more instant and inevitable.
Is it only a jostle of words after all, sparking
unexpectedly by the violence of their contact?
But that, I suppose, the stylist would retort is
just the point: it is this unprognosticable something struck out in the clash of language which
constitutes the celestial harmonies of style. At
any rate, whatever Pater was or was not aware
of till he had done it, we may take it for granted
that he found the result satisfactory and that
it is in so far significant of his own consciousness and of that which his work is likely to
induce in his readers.

In moments of listlessness when I abandon
myself, as I sometimes do, to the recollection
of my youth, what I regret most in such lacka-
daisical moods is the troop of involuntary
images, the idle pageantry of fancy and senti-

ment which used to occupy my attention to the exclusion of certain and definite ideas. My consciousness, as I look back upon it from the more or less settled footing of later life, I can but liken to a wintry New England night full of tremulous stars and constellations, arbitrarily grouped in curious and superficial patterns at the whim of the childish observer. Or again, it reminds me of the effect produced by pressing the eyeball and filling the vision with sparkling and incoherent fires of diversified shapes and colours. In some such vein as this I remember lying awake at night and listening to the high March winds or hearing the eaves drip monotonously in the April thaw or the spring rains rattle upon the roof or in summer the pounding of belated hoofs along the quiet country road. And I can remember too at the close of many a winter afternoon looking up from my reading, dazed with print, to see the evening sunlight climb the slope opposite my window; while in the same broken and desultory way I recall a bit of this book or that as it might be a half-familiar strain of music or a vague reflection in the corner of my eye.

So, as I remember these sensuous throngs of images, when some unexpected association revives them momentarily, they seem to have

given me the most exquisite pleasure that I
have ever known, much greater than that of
any voluntary or deliberate intellectual effort
— though their charm may be due in part to
the witchery of reminiscence. And all the while
my personal consistency must have been
mainly physiological. I know well enough that
it was always I — or psychologically should I
say "my me"? — who sat and registered these
incidents of vision. But my identity was due
apparently, not so much to my having thought
of them coherently, as to my having occupied
the same lodging and looked out of the same
window and seen the same landscape; the repetition of the same impressions may have supplied the ear marks by which I identified myself
from day to day, and not any conviction of
moral or spiritual integrity. And in support
of this conjecture I may mention the suspicion
of having lost myself among strange surroundings which would trouble and perplex me every
now and then. But with this exception my consciousness seems to have been like running
water, an inconstant current of ripples and
swirls and eddies.

Such is probably what William James would
have called a purely sensational existence or
life on the non-intellectual plane. But as I

remember it, it is almost identical with the state of mind induced by reading Pater. I seem to be drowsing again in my old room under the eaves or listening to the crisp frost crackling in the ground or watching from my window the early winter moonrise through the willows by the river or scenting once more the pungent earthy smell of Spring. Again the kaleidoscope is at my eye; again the multi-coloured pattern forms and scatters, reforms and disperses. Again for a few minutes I enjoy the old illusion, with all the allurements of bright glass and specious symmetry and disconnected succession.

This, then, is the point of Pater's style if I am successful in refurbishing my first impression. Whether it was the means of discovering his consciousness to himself as well as to others, is a moot question. But if you will turn to his own statements in the Preface to the " Renaissance " and in the Conclusion, you will agree, I think, that my account of its effect, so far from being overdrawn, represents pretty fairly what he himself valued and approved. So he speaks of the critic as regarding " all objects with which he has to do, all works of art, and the fairer forms of nature and human life, as powers or forces producing pleasurable sensa-

tions, each of a more or less pleasurable or
unique kind." And he refers to our experience
similarly as "a tremulous wisp constantly
reforming itself on the stream," and advises us,
as the sole good of life, to "catch at any exquisite passion . . . any stirring of the senses,
strange dyes, strange colours, and curious
odours." And in the same way what you recall
of his work are snatches of provocative and inconsequent imagery; as thus of Wordsworth:
— " He has a power likewise of realizing and
conveying to the consciousness of the reader,
abstract and elementary impressions — silence, darkness, absolute motionlessness; or
again, the whole complex sentiment of a particular place, the abstract expression of desola-
tion in the long white road, of peacefulness in a
particular folding of the hills." And to the same
effect I notice the trick of enumeration, which
he shares, for instance, with Walt Whitman, as
though he were a little dazzled and discon-
certed by his own sensations, like a man
brought of a sudden into a room full of mirrors
and lighted candles, who is reduced to the
childish expedient of pointing to this and that.
To see the subject as in itself it really is, to
relate one object with another, to evolve order
and system and principle from the combina-

tion — in short, to discover its plan or to organize the world around and within him, of this sort of effort Pater was incapable or disdainful. Nor did he find the function of style merely in the quickening of the imagination or the fancy as by a kind of involuntary reminiscence or reverie, but what is more momentous, in the deliberate incitement and sustentation of illusion.

In his essay " Style " prefixed to the volume of Appreciations already mentioned, he begins his discussion of the subject by virtually identifying literature — that is literature *par excellence,* belletrie — with art. The idea is French not English of course; but it is so familiar by this time that we need not linger over it. Only it is necessary to bear in mind that for Pater style and literature are synonymous — at least style is the fulfilment, the consummation of literature. " Just in proportion as the writer's aim consciously or unconsciously comes to be the transcribing, not of the world, not of mere fact, but of his sense of it, he becomes an artist; his work *fine* art." Or as Maupassant puts it, a little more emphatically, in the introduction to " Pierre et Jean " : — " Each of us creates for himself an illusion of the world, which is poetic or sentimental or joyous or melancholic

or unclean or lugubrious, according to his temperament, and the writer has no other mission
than to reproduce faithfully this illusion." The
notion is clear — in fact, it has become rather
trite. For the reader at least the essence of
literature is illusion. And when we think what
consciousness would be without language, how
inchoate and vague, is it not evident that for the
writer too style must serve in somewhat the
same capacity, if not as the principal, at all
events as the actuary of illusion?

And further, " as the writer's aim," to return
to Pater, " comes to be the transcribing, not of
the world . . . but of his sense of it, he becomes
an artist, his work *fine* art; and good art . . .
in proportion to the truth of his presentment
of that sense. . . . Truth! there can be no
merit, no craft at all without that. And further,
all beauty is in the long run only *fineness* of
truth, or what we call expression, the finer accommodation of speech to that vision within."
In a word, truth, then, is fidelity to illusion.
And may I call the definition to the attention
of the philosophers as well as the *literati?*
Truth has nothing to do with one's sense of
fact or with the character of the vision as such
— that may be what it will, " poetic or sentimental or joyous or melancholic or unclean or

lugubrious." Truth concerns style solely in its relation not to reality but to illusion; truth is illusion.

In view of the tenets of the artistic school to which Pater belonged the definition is ingenious. But as a criterion of anything in particular it threatens on examination to become rather embarrassing even to the irresponsible artist who is ready for anything with a little paradoxical pungency about it. Since our only means of getting at the author's mind is his language and we are therefore unable to compare directly his consciousness with his expression of it, we must either abandon the search for reality altogether or else we must accept every form and mode of expression at its face value and on its own recognizance, in which case any test or criterion is idle and irrelevant.

In the latter alternative, which is the only one open to us practically, for the former would disqualify literature completely in leading us to distrust everything an author might tell us — in the latter alternative, I say, since the relation as such between thought and expression has broken down irrestorably with the elimination of reality, we are reduced to defining style as an absolute. But in consideration, again, of the fact that we know nothing of the writer's vision but his expression of it, which we have just defined as truth, we must consistently define style as both truth and illusion also. Whence it follows that for art truth and illusion are indiscernible and hence identical.

The consequence is interesting; it explains so many of the more modern artistic movements for which *l'art pour l'art* is remotely as well as proximately responsible. It is in some such course as this, I fancy, that art and literature — particularly the former, if we may institute a distinction so abhorrent to the principles that we are discussing — it was in some such course that art began and continued to lose its hold of reality until it has finally ceased in extreme cases to be representative or " idolatrous " at all. Hence the curious heresy whereby the plastic arts are supposed to create their own objects — for example, those vicious what-you-may-call-'ems and obscene thing-'em-bobs that we have become more or less familiar with, especially in sculpture — or do they only look worse in statuary? — though painting is not without its own enormities either. And by a parity of reasoning the pre-eminence of style is to be accounted for, no doubt, as it is itself the special construct or creation of literature, in

view of the irrelevance for criticism of any consideration of subject or theme. It looks from
the entrance like a blind alley.

And now for the application. Since style is
wholly factitious and opaque, inasmuch as it
is patterned upon an illusion at once personal
and unique, it will neither possess qualities of
its own such as are or would be proper to a
medium of representation, like clearness; nor
will it acquire the qualities of an object or a
matter to which it recognizes no obligations or
which it altogether ignores, being ultimately
its own object and matter; but what qualities
it does own, it must derive from its creator, the
" artist " or illusionist alone. In the abstract
they fall, according to Pater, into three classes
— scholarship, mind, and soul. And upon the
first two I will comment briefly.

Scholarship! The conjunction is disconcert-
ing. " The literary artist is of necessity a
scholar, and in what he proposes to do will
have in mind, first of all, the scholar and the
scholarly conscience." From the date of Pater's
education, however, as well as from the context
it becomes evident that what he has in mind
can not be the banausic or trade scholarship to
which we have become accustomed of late years,
the scholarship of the Teuto-American univer-

sity which fraternizes so kindly with illiteracy
that they might be taken for blood-brothers.
What Pater is thinking of is the liberal scholarship, the traditional humanistic scholarship
of England and France, which based upon a
study of letters and literature was in itself a
patron of discrimination as well as learning.
"Science and good taste" — to use his own
terms in spite of the misleading connotation attaching at present to the former — knowledge
and judgment are the qualities of style for
which Pater looks to the scholar. " He will feel
the obligation not of the laws only, but of those
affinities, those mere preferences, of his language, which through the associations of literary history have become a part of its nature,"
while " his punctilious observance of the proprieties of his medium will diffuse through all
he writes a general air of sensibility, of refined
usage." — As for mind, Pater detects it " in
the critical tracing out of that conscious artistic structure, and the pervading sense of it
as we read " which is " one of the greatest pleasures of really good prose literature " and for
that matter, " of poetic literature too, for, in
truth, the kind of constructive intelligence here
supposed is one of the forms of imagination "
— though in point of fact, when we come to

look at them closely, these traceries as illustrated in the essay appear the affair of syntax and rhetoric, of transitions and verbal cues fully as much as intellectual design or preconception.

But no matter for that; in their general idea there is no intelligible difficulty about mind and scholarship. It is when he approaches the seat of soul that Pater begins to shroud himself in the vagueness appropriate to the hierophant of a mystery. "By soul," he intimates, "the literary artist " — mark the words " literary artist," enough in themselves to curdle the blood of the profane — " reaches us, somewhat capriciously perhaps, one and not another, through vagrant sympathy and a kind of immediate contact." And again he speaks of it as a kind of " ' elective affinity ' . . . working in all cases by an immediate sympathetic contact." It is all very bewildering; and if it were not for Maupassant, whose brutality makes short work of verbal subtleties and refinements, the riddle might remain unread. In his introduction to the "Lettres de Gustave Flaubert à George Sand " he seems to be on the same track himself. "Words," he affirms, " have a soul. The majority of readers and even of writers require of them nothing more than a sense. But it is necessary, just the same, to discover and bring out this soul which is revealed in their contact with other words, and which illumines and transfigures certain books with ineffable splendour." And further, " There is, in the affinities and combinations of language as written by some men, an evocation of a whole world of poetry, which the worldlings are unable to perceive or divine. If you wish to speak to them on such a subject, they are vexed, they reason, argue, discuss, cry out, deny, and ask you to prove it." And finally, " Educated and intelligent men and writers are astonished when you speak to them of this *mystery* [the italics are Maupassant's] of which they are ignorant. They smile and shrug their shoulders. But what difference does it make? They do not understand; that is all. You might just as well talk music to people who have no ear." And he goes on to draw his well known portrait of Flaubert as " the patient colossus," savagely rubbing his words together, " red in the face, with swollen cheeks and neck, his muscles as tense as a straining athlete's," in the hope, somehow or other, sooner or later, of eliciting this celestial spark, " which animates literature with a soul " [*qui met une ame dans les œuvres*] the very portrait upon which Pater relies for his eulogy of " the martyr of literary style " with which he concludes his essay.

This, then, as far as I can explain or even understand it, is what I have already spoken of as the æsthetico-literary mysticism which seems to clothe Pater's and Maupassant's conception of style as illusion. And yet in spite of all that we owe it — for we do owe it a good deal for all its absurdities — I can not help suspecting a mistake somewhere. No author or " artist " is a very safe critic of his own or any other artist's performance. And while both Pater and Maupassant pretend to view Flaubert with a respect amounting to veneration, they have, it seems to me, completely misrepresented his meaning, if Maupassant, that is to say, has reported him correctly.

" Having, besides, laid down this truth that there are not in the world two grains of sand, two specks, two hands, or two noses exactly alike, he made me describe, in a few phrases, a being or an object in such a manner as clearly to particularize it and distinguish it from all other beings or objects of the same race or the same species.

" ' When you pass,' he used to say, ' a green grocer seated at his shop-door, a janitor smok-

ing his pipe, a stand of hackney-coaches, show
me that grocer and that janitor, their attitude,
their whole physical appearance, embracing
likewise, as indicated by the skilfulness of the
picture, their whole moral nature so that I can
not confound them with any other grocer or
any other janitor: make me see, in a word, that
a certain cab-horse does not resemble the fifty
others that follow or precede it.' "

The passage has been quoted so often that I
should hesitate to repeat it, were it not for the
fact that its purport appears to have escaped
the penetration of the cult. As a matter of fact
it agrees much better with Aristotle's doctrine
of imitation than with Maupassant's and
Pater's illusionism; its whole weight impends
upon the side of representation.

It is in this light, at all events, that Brunetière sees Flaubert; and in correction of what
I am bound to consider a critical error I will
quote after Brunetière three excerpts from
" Madame Bovary " with his comments. I can
not expect, of course, to reproduce Flaubert in
English; but my translations, however halting,
should be near enough to serve the purpose.

" It was thawing. In the yard the trees oozed
with sap, and the snow was melting on the

roofs. She stood on the sill and opened her umbrella. The sunlight, filtering through the dove-coloured silk, irradiated her fair complexion with flickering reflections. She smiled at the genial warmth — while the water dripped monotonously upon the taut silk, drop by drop." —

"The sky was turning blue, the leaves were still; there were wide spaces covered with heather all in flower, and patches of violets alternated with masses of trees, gray, tawny, and gold according to the variety of the foliage. Often there was a little flutter of wings rustling under the leaves or a hoarse soft cry of crows flying about among the oaks." —

"Night spread gently around them; patches of shadow covered the foliage. Emma, her eyes half-closed, breathed the fresh air with a sigh. Now and again some creature of the night, a hedgehog or a weasel, starting on the chase, disturbed the leaves, or a ripe peach fell singly from the trellis."

Of these quotations, after citing them as characteristic of their author, Brunetière remarks as follows: —

"In these three cases it is a question of finding for a certain season of the year, for a certain hour of the day or night, the exact index or sign that will give to the vagueness of a general description the accent of individuality. The murmurs of a May night are not the sounds of an October day; the silence of an August noon is not the silence of a December midnight. . . And in this respect . . . you see that the whole value of the description lies in the final trait, in this imperceptible touch — the water dripping on the taut silk, the cry of the crows flying about in the oaks, the sound of the peach loosened from the trellis."

In other words, if Brunetière is right, Flaubert's aim was to make true, not curious. Such is his dream of the impersonal style, *le style impersonnel,* a style which should be, as it were, the very thing itself in words, the linguistic image or duplication of the object. Taken in this sense style would be form, the actualization of the idea in another matter, a complete and perhaps a higher, because a more essential, reality in itself. But this is very far from Pater's illusionism or even Maupassant's. And so I say that in fathering upon Flaubert the ingenious literary animism which endows language with a " soul " apart from its sense, he has not only done his " master " an injustice but has paved the way for the heresy of an art not merely unrepresentative but unintelligible.

De Quincey's "Dream Fugue"

ACCORDING to De Quincey himself his originality as an author very nearly comports with his having invented or discovered a kind of prose of his own such as is illustrated by "The Dream Fugue" or the "Suspiria de Profundis." It is a prose distinguished externally by an extravagant use of rhythm and cadence, of phonic and tonal effects; internally by imaginative and emotional, even hysterical exaltation. That De Quincey on occasion practised such a prose with remarkable success, is a fact; that he originated it, is a mistake. For these properties of spirit and style are recognizable in seventeenth century prose; indeed, they are everywhere characteristic of elementary or only partially differentiated prose — prose that has not yet disentangled itself by a critical rectification from poetry and eloquence. In one sense English has never completely outgrown these vestigia — save momentarily as in the Age of Anne; so that it is fair enough to say that formally such prose is in the English tradition. It is the prose of Sir Thomas Browne and Burke; it is the prose of English oratory — a pattern upon which English prose, as De Quincey himself acknowledges, has always been too prone to model itself. In sober truth, then, what De Quincey accomplished in these respects was hardly more at most than a revival or restoration.

And yet in one particular he is perhaps entitled to take rank in English as an innovator though like all the modern romanticists he is anticipated in a way by the great heresiarch Rousseau. In many instances these rhapsodical pieces, upon which he prided himself particularly, purport to be dreams or visions. They emancipate themselves at the outset from every obligation of regular and rational discourse. They renounce, to all intents and purposes, the restraint of logical coherence and consecutiveness and acknowledge allegiance only to the suggestions of a subject essentially wilful and vagrant. Singularly enough in the case of a man who boasts that from his birth he was made an intellectual creature they repudiate the principle of the logos; their law is the law of psychological association or reverie. Their literary merit consists, in modern cant, in the rhythmization of emotion. In this respect, whether of set purpose or not, they naturalize in English the ideal dream economy exploited by Novalis and his circle and in this way offer a convenient means of studying in our own language one of the characteristics of continental Romanticism.

To understand the peculiar bent or twist given it by De Quincey one must recall certain circumstances of his life and character. The story of his addiction to laudanum has been told so circumstantially in " The Confessions of an English Opium Eater " that it need scarcely be referred to, much less repeated. His bickerings with Coleridge over the latter's comparative unregeneracy, the anecdote of the decanter of laudanum from which the guests at his table must be warned lest they mistake it for port or sherry, his complaints of his inability at the height of his excesses to cope with any subject less trivial than political economy — these are the superficial humours of his vice and need touching only with the flippant finger of gossip. The gravamen of the matter is the literary inspiration that he found in the characteristic opium dream or vision.

How documentary these set pieces of his, remains an open question; we are none too certain of the accuracy of what purports to be the

history of his traffickings with the drug. But
there is no doubt that they are reminiscent of
the kind of thing that troubled his consciousness on the occasion of his dissipations; they
are intended to poetize experience. In many
cases it is the bare suggestion, the mood or atmosphere, the intoxication itself which is borrowed. For the possibilities compare Stevenson's " A Chapter on Dreams "; though there
is this to be said for Stevenson that whereas his
literary activity apparently consists in an effort
to rationalize his visionary material, De Quincey is always busy to the contrary effect in an
attempt to de-rationalize his still further. But
in the case of " The Dream Fugue " it is the
entire theme. And what makes this particular
effusion so illuminative is the fact that the incident from which it derives has been developed
circumstantially in the preceding sections of
" The English Mail Coach."

To be sure, its machinery is not that of the
waking reason, or for that matter of the literary
consciousness at all, as the names *dream* and
fugue signify. But just as it is possible to account for the ravings of delirium more or less
by a knowledge of the patient's previous states
of mind, so is it possible, too, to explain after a
fashion the composition of " The Dream

Fugue " by a reference to the author's auto-
biography. In themselves the colliding ships and
the sinking maidens and the whirling coaches
and the reverberating cathedrals are meaningless; they are only symbols, their sense is to be
sought in the preceding descriptions. In both
these accounts, " The Glory of Motion " and
" The Vision of Sudden Death " — which together with " The Dream Fugue " itself compose the trilogy of " The Mail Coach " — the
impression of breathless velocity is inherent in
the subject itself and is accountable for one of
the main moments of the " Fugue " as visual-
ized in these fleeting vessels, fleeing female figures — " woman's Ionic form " — and speed-
ing cars. While interfused with such images of
that one simple irrational emotion is traceable
an equally somnambulistic sense of victory or
triumph, typified by the exulting organs and
the towering minsters, and explicable as a
reminiscence of Waterloo — the dissemination
of the news by mail coach, whereon De Quincey
happened to be a passenger, constituting as in
reverie the associative principle. These two ab-
stracts or ghosts of experience — aptly *reve-
nants* in French — appear and reappear in one
guise and another during the course of the
rhapsody in a manner somewhat like the motifs

of a fugue, much more than "concretions in discourse." And if it be remembered that De Quincey was more or less under the spell of opium on the occasions when these impressions were formed, the vividness and incoherence with which they are presented in the " Fugue " will be comprehensible. They probably haunted his drugged slumbers as they do this prose-poem of his — how far we have travelled since this obsolescent word was a neologism! — in partnership with the shadowy episode which supplies the third motif — the apprehension of imminent disaster and paralytic expectancy — and which after all is the matrix or mother of the " Fugue."

Of this incident "The Vision of Sudden Death " purports to be an account. How literal or accurate is of no great consequence. It is at least an intelligible composition, and serves by comparison to illustrate the disintegration to which De Quincey has submitted the discourse of reason in the preparation of these effusions.

According to his story, then, it was night; and fortified for his journey by an unusually stout dose of laudanum, he sat in his outside seat by the driver, contemplating the unrolling panorama of the road, his senses sharpened but his activities benumbed, his powers of will and motion inhibited by the influence of the opiate, which was already beginning to work its customary effect. Suddenly, as they were driving at full speed down a long straight tree-lined avenue, which is recognizable as one of the more persistent types of the " Fugue," he saw before them in the road immediately in the way of the coach a light cart or carriage containing a young man and woman. It was impossible to arrest the horses, which were plunging on at a break-neck gallop; it was equally impossible to turn aside without wrecking the coach. And besides, the driver was to all appearance quite unaware of the danger, as were also the occupants of the carriage. It seemed as though collision were unavoidable — as though the frail cart must inevitably be run down and shattered, and the two unsuspecting lives which occupied it be obliterated with it.

As for De Quincey himself, playing the part of chorus to the microcosmic cataclysm, he was powerless to move or cry out, either to warn his driver or the pair in jeopardy, or to grasp at the reins and assume the *rôle* of providence himself. But although motionless, he was by no means senseless. The opium which had palsied his initiative had exasperated his sensibilities. In an instant as immeasurable as an eternity he saw and felt, as though it were immediate, the whole catastrophe — the shivered carriage, the bruised and mangled bodies of its owners — in a horror of apprehension like a nightmare. The affair, indeed, may have been hallucinatory. Quite possibly the speed of the coach and the sight of an obstruction had been sufficient of themselves to suggest to De Quincey's quickening brain the notion of a calamity which existed in fact only for his over-wrought imagination. My suspicions are perhaps unworthy in view of his last eloquent description of that " little cany carriage," trembling and shivering from a glancing blow that it had all but avoided, and of " the lady " as " she rose and sank upon her seat, sank and rose, threw up her arms wildly to heaven, clutched at some visionary object in the air, fainting, praying, raving, despairing." And then, to adapt his language, in the twinkling of an eye his flying horses had borne him to the termination of the umbrageous aisle, and the turn of the road had carried the scene out of his eyes in an instant and swept it into his dreams forever.

Such is the third moment or motif of the rhapsody — this sense of anguished expectation and calamity. Like the others it has its source in actuality and is capable of intelligible

statement — which, indeed, they all three re-
ceive in the earlier portions of " The Mail
Coach," before they suffer their final transmu-
tation in the " insubstantial pageant " of the
" Fugue." Both these two preceding papers,
" The Glory of Motion " and " The Vision of
Sudden Death," are good plain straightforward prose — allowance made for what some
one has called De Quincey's rigmarole; they
deal with experience as digested and assimi-
lated by the mind; their subjects are concrete
and palpable, their trains of thought consecutive. In " The Dream Fugue," on the contrary,
emotion has broken away from the concretions
in which at first it inhered and has become a
kind of abstraction without conceptual or
factual support, incapable of representation
proper, realizable at all only by means of a more
or less arbitrary symbolization, a sort of astral
literary body, shunning " the light of common
day " with its logical and chronological exigen-
cies, and susceptible only to the incoherences
and aberrations of " the vision splendid," as
Wordsworth has it, " the glory and the freshness of a dream." — But every one knows
" The Mail Coach "; it is " stock." And yet in
a comparison of the several parts no one, it
appears, has paid any particular attention to

this symptomatic resolution of thought into imagery, with its unavowed but implicit nostalgia of the vaguer, more elementary and primitive consciousness, and even, it may be, of that undifferentiated "sensational continuum " — the term is Dr. Ward's — from which our intellectual life has been so painfully and precariously developed, and to which, at least on the artistic side of our activity, we now seem possessed to return.

What has saved literature — or rather, what did save literature so long from this mental and moral dissolution was, curiously enough, its mechanism. The ideas expressed might be ever so romantic; but the necessity of logical coherence continued to keep literature more or less rational, whatever the sentiments of its writers. Music, for example, recognizes such an obligation least, and is the most romantic, as it is the most formless of all the arts. But literature, until this connection was broken up, was doomed to remain an imperfectly romantic art. Attempts to this end had been made; in Germany Tieck had written his " Prinz Zerbino " and Friedrich Schlegel his " Lucinde." Whether De Quincey was acquainted with these experiments I can not say. But their result in any case was merely topsy-turvydom —

a shuffling and displacement of parts integral enough in themselves — and so failed to vitiate the essential consistency of discourse. While the fragment which Schlegel affected was only inchoation — abortive? yes — but not dissolution, an incomplete but not a rotten thread. On the whole it is to De Quincey that the honour belongs of having sapped the vital integrity of composition and shown the feasibility of a complete abrogation of the *ratio* in discourse, so assimilating writing to musing and the art of literature to the art of music. Of course, he has been outdistanced since, as we who have lived to see the humiliation of grammar and syntax in the name of liberty need no reminder. Nevertheless his " Dream Fugue " and his " Suspiria " entitle him to the glory of the innovation.

Upon a discussion of free verse I have no mind to enter — it is condemned out of its own mouth — or of prose-poetry, which was another thing altogether. Under the latter head, however, I should have to do justice to De Quincey's respect for rhythm despite his sins against the logic of composition. At least he has refrained from that breaking up of the language of emotion which is the suicidal impulse of *vers libre*. By this one virtue, if no other,

De Quincey's effusions still retain their place in the English literary tradition, for all their intellectual delinquencies, along with Sir Thomas Browne's " Urn Burial " and " Religio Medici." There is still something informing about the very resonance of his periods like the vibrations of the bow which shifts the scattered sand on the metal plate into distinct and symmetrical patterns. It is only sentiment, to be sure, loose and diffusive stuff itself; but it is not quite chaotic, at least it simulates a structure or idea.

Ibsen

FOR any sort of superiority above the dull dead level of inanimate matter nature cherishes an implacable hatred. While condemned, by some imperative law of becoming, to the conception of higher and higher forms of existence, yet on the whole spontaneous side of her activity she seems, in revenge for the anguish of her enforced travail, to contrive for the extinction of her offspring, so initiating the eternal contradiction of growth and decay. Wasteful, faithless, and cunning, she has sown in every aggregation of organized matter the germ of dissolution, rooted deep in the constitution of the protoplasmic jelly and spreading up into consciousness in a thousand suicidal impulses of license and revolt. Not content with this act of perfidy, she has arrayed one individual, one society, one civilization against another in an endless war of extermination from the lowest instinct of brute rivalry to the most subtle refinement of modern competition so that the very condition of existence for one is the extinction of others

and the single indispensable institution of society is the slaughter-house. For the species, as
a matter of fact, she cares as little as for the
individual for what is palæontology but a record of her cancellations? The higher the form,
just so much the more does she begrudge it
being which may surpass her own so that the
type of greatest instability and impermanence
is exactly that rarest and most precious of all,
the human spirit with the fruit it has produced
at once in imitation and in defiance of nature
— even when as here man has set himself
against the great leveller for his own preser-
vation and protection.

Among all the agents of this reactionary impulse of nature the romantic naturalist is the
most insidious. In the ceaseless duel between
genesis and corruption it is with his mother's
darker, more disastrous moods that he sympa-
thizes. Partially civilized and educated, the
man of a half-truth, with the tremendous
vigour and assurance that belong to this character, he sides with the crude Titanic forces of
disorder and annihilation. He is usually ignorant of his own significance and imagines himself to be reforming, constructing, creating,
while all the time, with the dust of demolition
in his eyes, he is scattering broadcast the seeds

of dissolution and decay. As with his mother so with him, it is the noblest and best that excites his blind animosity. Inevitably, when such an one writes, it is of what he thinks most — of dark untoward things, of mind in eclipse, of the obscure suggestions of derangement and confusion with which his brain riots, implanted by his parent at the origins of life.

Of Ibsen's " art " in the narrower sense that limits the extension of the term to technique, we have heard many wonders. — " Enfin Malherbe vint." — He has revolutionized dramatic method. He has scrapped the conventional French model of the mid-century, though what he first learned from it his flatterers have little or nothing to say. He has done away forever with such clumsy makeshifts as monologue and soliloquy. In epitomizing the issues of a long series of events or a course of time in a single critical situation after such a fashion as to reflect its causes and foreshadow its consequences — in " putting the spectator to begin with at the post where the race is to be decided," — he has displaced the sprawling old action with one so compact, instant, and vivid as perforce to recall — God save the mark! — the intention and pertinence of Attic tragedy. In short, he has set the action right side up at last and in the stead of the horizontal has established the perpendicular drama.

But for all that his theatre, as the French would say, is not quite faultless, whether or no its failings are the defects of its qualities. In particular it suffers from its abuse of duologue and its addiction to reminiscence and retrospection. The stove and the sofa — when I think of Ibsen, these are the symbols. There are next to no minor characters; at most there are supernumeraries who fringe the plot without much affecting it. Every play is a duel. Its dimensions are so limited that it comes to resemble a desert island with its own scanty quota of shipwrecked mariners, whose distracted ringleaders have no more to do in their appalling isolation and inanity than to revive some old half-forgotten quarrel so remote and wraithlike as to seem quite factitious, were it not for the artificial provocation to which they are subjected. In this way the interest, as a rule, arises less from the exhibition of a dramatic present than from the disclosure of a narrative past, the story of a bygone. But a complicated exposition is much more embarrassing than a complicated intrigue; the latter is at least aboveboard and at the level of the stage. And it may be for this reason that the Ibsen *dénoue-*

ment has somewhat the air of a mirage, the refraction of another clime and time — something subliminal and visionary and necromantic, like a conjurer's trick.

But aside from the naïveté of confounding art with technique — I am conservative or reactionary, no doubt; but I have a notion that the problem of drama is neither staging nor setting nor even lighting — the most portentous phenomenon of Ibsenism has been its infectiousness. The force of the drama is in its ideas in spite of the fact that the dramatist is not in the first instance a philosopher but an alchemist. Like the plant he draws his alimentation from his surroundings, the soil and the atmosphere about him, and transmutes it into a various foliage for the appropriation of his patrons. Psychologically, I suppose, he must be classed as a behaviorist; his characters are what they do. At all events his ideas are never free or inorganic, but are always to be found in the vital combinations of action and character. Now, it is frequently said — and it is true too — that the significantly Ibsenesque figure is woman. She is his favourite for she is of the same descent and parentage. In spite of her affectations and disguises she is more " instinctive " and impulsive, she is less " spoilt "

by civilization than man. Her higher attributes
are all gifts of her lovers — particularly her
poetry and her " spirituality." Herself she is,
as nearly as can be, nature incarnate — a fact
which accounts for her romantic apotheosis. In
contrast with the futility of the male — the
abortive genius who is Lövberg or Solness or
Rosmer, the victim of reflection — her autom-
atism makes her appear a marvel of resource
and vigour. On the whole, she is well described
in the words of one of M. Janet's neuropathic
patients — " Madeleine " he calls her : " Il faut
pour retrouver ma liberté que j'arrive, malgrè
tout le monde, à faire des choses extraordinaires
. . . Il faut que je parvienne à soulever le
monde, à moi toute seule! Il faut que j'impose ma volonté aux autres! " This is the
formula, " pour retrouver ma liberté," the ac-
cents are unmistakable, " il faut que j'impose
ma volonté aux autres." To be sure, it is a *crise;*
but in the transport of the paroxysm she has
all the imperiousness of the malady of which
she is the victim.

I say " she," for just as Ibsen never succeeded
with more than one kind of man, so he was
limited as " creator " to a single woman; others
do not count. Hilda, Hedda, Rebecca, Nora,
Ellida — they would all, like " Madeleine," re-

cover their liberty (from what? discipline? authority?) by some deed so extravagant as to shake the firmament — and shock the respectable. It is one and the same woman at different ages and stages of arrested development — or rather of retrogression toward that "divine mother" nature which is the adoration of the romantic. All that changes is the mood, the convulsion that accompanies or provokes the catastrophe. In default of the genuine productivity, the lavishness of the highest genius, this is what makes Ibsen so interesting — that it is possible to follow so clearly from play to play, as from one clinic to another, the course of her degeneration, through what M. Janet would call, I believe, its egoistic and "asseritive" levels with Hilda and Hedda, and something very like mental debility with Ellida — the order is not chronological — into the imbecility and even idiocy of the final period personified in Irene.

But literary criticism is not yet abnormal psychology though so many of our modern authors have been doing their best to make it such. To set the term provisionally at "Master Builder Solness," beyond which anything that can be called character or personality, and drama with them, begin to recede and dissolve

into the fogs of instinctivism, primitivism — or
what not? — the notion of her who was to become Hilda Wangel must have entered her
creator's head some time before the period of
what Mr. Archer calls the "plays of pure
psychology" — those, that is to say, which begin with "The Lady from the Sea." Already in
"The League of Youth," which heads the
dramas distinguished by the critic aforesaid as
"social," Selma is a recognizable adumbration
of Nora. To be sure, Selma has little to say;
but in what little she does say, even in her
silent protest she strikes, however quaveringly,
the note of that blind, purposeless revolt
against reason and order, tradition and experience which was to characterize all her successors "social" or "psychological." She is not so
mutinous as Nora — nor is she so passionate
and fatuous as Hedda, or so evasive and im-
penitent as Hilda. But while less distinct to her
maker, she is in herself a more definite, if less
"thrilling" character; she is more rational.
She has at least the advantage of knowing in a
way what she wants inasmuch as she represents
a more advanced or "sublimated," a less retrograde type of consciousness. For it is to be
noticed that as the character becomes clearer
to the author, it becomes more and more enig-

matical to itself; in fact, it is not so much the character that develops as the disease.

The conception, once sown in Ibsen's brain, germinated rapidly, until it unfolded into that ambiguous elemental we know as Hilda Wangel. I may be wrong, but by what light I have I take Hilda rather than Hedda to be the consummate Ibsenitish woman, though for my own part I prefer Hedda, she is so diabolic. But that is the point. If Hilda is less malignant, it is because she has retreated further toward the simple "innocency of nature," that state of infantile blessedness so admired of Wordsworth. Her adolescence is symptomatic. She is neither wholly girl nor wholly woman — full of curiosity and *velléité* but hardly capable of passion; restless, "dreamy," and inconsequential, a puzzle to herself, a tantalizing and unsettling apparition to others. To a mental equilibrist, in particular, like Solness there is a peculiar vertiginous fascination about this sensuous immaturity and emotional instability. It is the secret of her provocation. She can hardly be thought of as beautiful, this epigone of the fiords — "after the flesh's kind" she is only Ellida's step-child, but she is her daughter *im Geiste,* in the nomenclature of the earlier romanticists, though there is perhaps as much of the gnome in her as of the undine. If anything, one might suppose that the incubation of that brood of morbid fancies hatched during the endless winter months in those stove-choked rooms which had seen her successive dramatic avatars, would have begun by this time to find some sort of facial cast and expression for itself.

But all this is beside the mark. Ibsen's strength does not lie in the delineation of any superiority or excellence of body or mind. On the contrary. While classic tragedy — and I use the word *classic* very broadly, almost in the sense of traditional — while such tragedy has been as a rule a tragedy of excess, of the abuse of some great but ill regulated or unbalanced power; Ibsen's, on the other hand, is a tragedy of defect. His men are all weaklings. Where is his Othello or Cinna or Orestes? Between his vapouring geniuses and Hamlet there is, perhaps, a deceptive resemblance; but which of them shows anything like Hamlet's penetration into the characters and motives of those about him? He is at least aware of himself and his situation and retains the ability, if not to act, at all events to react. But Ibsen's is a feminist drama and liable to the frailties of the sex. In this respect, of all the great drama with which we are invited to rank it, it runs the nearest parallel, no doubt, with Racine's. But where is the counterpart of Roxane or Hermione or even Phèdre? Its fatality is either a *malaise* as in "Hedda Gabler" or a *défaillance* as in "Solness" or a misgiving as in "Rosmersholm." Even Ellida escapes destruction rather by a kind of delinquency or indisposition than by any exertion or intention of her own, nervous or otherwise. While as for poor Irene, the ultimate letter of the Ibsen script, what is she but a symbol of the dissolution which overtakes the "art" that seeks to immortalize the infirmities and distempers of humanity?

Such is the Ibsen drama; and such is the explanation of its vogue — it is so agreeable with the complexion of its time. Consider our "advanced" ideas as they are coming to embody themselves in our Western institutions — woman-suffrage, divorce, prohibition, pacifism. These are not the counsels of strength, of a robust and vigorous society. Rather, they appear the last desperate recourses of futility; they reek of sentimentality, emasculation, sottishness, incontinence. And their irrational character is evident in the fact that they encourage and proscribe one vice and another with complete indiscrimination. After their own fashion they realize the general deterioration of civilization as diagnosed by Ibsen in the degeneration of the individual. In fact, they are so far prolongations of Ibsenism as to have invested their augur with the reputation of a hierophant — this is, indeed, the genuine Ibsen symbolism or allegory. Dean Inge has spoken of the United States as an " ice-water-drinking gynæcocracy "; but what more staring example of masochism than that which Ibsen has provided in his abasement and humiliation of the male and of the hardier elements of society? For that matter, what is democracy itself but an attempt to capitalize inferiority? How does it manifest itself as it proceeds but as a progressive degradation?

We all have our cellarage, I dare say, which seems just now in imminent danger of being turned over to the cultivation of fungi exclusively. Personally, I am not insensible, I confess, to the sorcery of Ibsen and the spell which he and his like exert over the denizens of our under-world; no doubt, they are able to conjure the ghost of our savage and even bestial ancestry — the natural man. I remember in particular reading " Hedda Gabler " when it first came out in German translation; it haunted me for a day and a night, and that is no little while in the case of a desultory reader — as well as

"When We Dead Awaken." And I should like to edge in a word of protest against the general denigration of the latter play. Granted, it is not very dramatic; but then I often find it difficult to see the dramatic in Ibsen anyway — at least in reading — in "The Lady from the Sea," for instance, and in "Solness" and "Little Eyolf" and "John Gabriel Borkman"; so that I sometimes catch myself wondering whether the great playwright is so very great a dramatist after all. But dramatic or not, "When We Dead Awaken" is extremely Ibsenesque at least; it belongs unmistakably in the series as "epilogue" or final term. It is identified by the analysis and "exposition," the "eavesdropping" and story-telling that mark all the later plays. And above all, it has the peculiar lyricism and elegiacism, the Ibsenesque narcosis that passes for "mysticism" and "supernaturalism" — in larger dosage but no less characteristic on that account.

Be this as it may; the most obvious test of the timeliness or "actuality" of an art is its imitation. It is no exaggeration to say that since 1890 there is hardly a drama which has escaped the contagion of Ibsenism. Its success has been amazing, a *succès de fou*. And yet at what a price has it been bought! Classic art at least was not an engine of demolition. It was man's supreme attempt to order the welter and jumble of experience, to reconcile the discrepancies which the birth of consciousness has brought into the world, to organize for himself, in spite of the grudge of nature, a little island in the midst of the flux, a human polity amid the moral anarchy which surrounds him. Its essence is measure and form. But this is what the romanticist, especially the naturalist, can not or will not understand. Down through all the successive strata of his being his atavistic promptings stir him to rake over the phosphorescent refuse and corruption of creation in the hope of turning up the little blue flower of pre-rational felicity, "*die verschollne blaue Blume.*"

It is in some such way as this, I suppose, that art has lost the sense of its mission and has become with science the twin superstition of democracy, whose temples, the "movie-theatre" and the laboratory, occupy the extremities of the market-place, or in current diction, the civic centre of our culture. That the laboratory is fast becoming a mere adjunct to the shop or factory, while the "movie" is scarcely distinguishable from a sort of establishment it were better not to refer to at all —

this association appears to injure their popularity but little. What may be the particular idolatry — "ideal," I should say — of science at the present moment it is difficult to decide — it harbours so many strange bed-fellows — rubber, perhaps, synthetic rubber, to judge from the oracle of democracy, the newspaper, or not impossibly gas, "the bringer of peace unto mortals." But of the reigning divinity of the "lot" and the "studio" there can be little or no question. Call her Lubricity with Matthew Arnold or Libertina with Swinburne or what you will, there is evidently nothing to be expected of our art — "artistry" as we like to name it — in mediation of the two extremes, the "vitalistic" emotionalism or "intuitivism" and the "mechanistic" rationalism, between which our minds are distracted and our civilization is disrupting. In reality, our art has thrown her influence into the other camp; and if not frankly immoralist, for English art is bound to be more or less hypocritical, is at least quite as amoralist as science. I apologize for the jargon; but our vocabulary is not all that has suffered from that discrediting of humanism which is one of the feats of popular education. Their sons inherit them; and in the anti-intellectualist plight in which we find ourselves, since the dogma of progress must be retained at any cost, we have hit upon no less ingenious an expedient for reconciling the progeny of Darwin and Rousseau than that of confounding evolution and progressive degeneration.